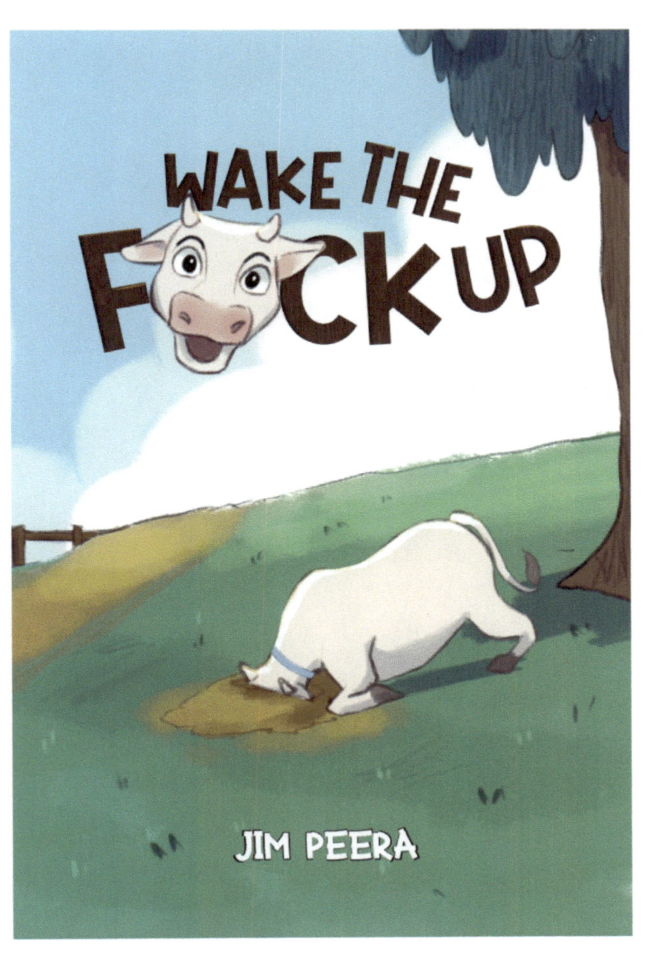

JIM PEERA

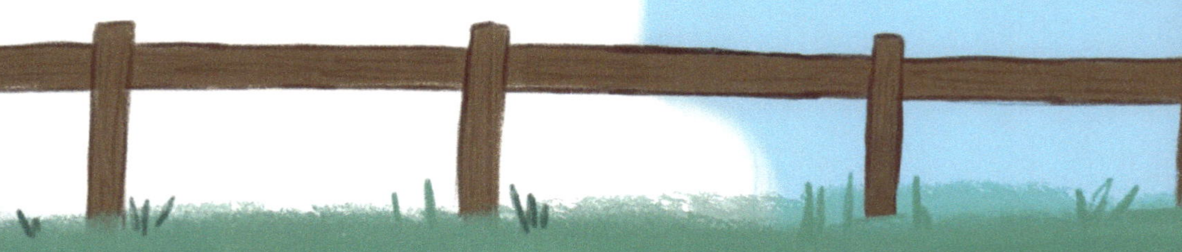

ISBN: 978-1-7375950-5-2

Printed in the United States of America

Dedicated to that mother and father
who helped create a powerful
one-of-a-kind miracle of life
on this beautiful planet:

YOU!

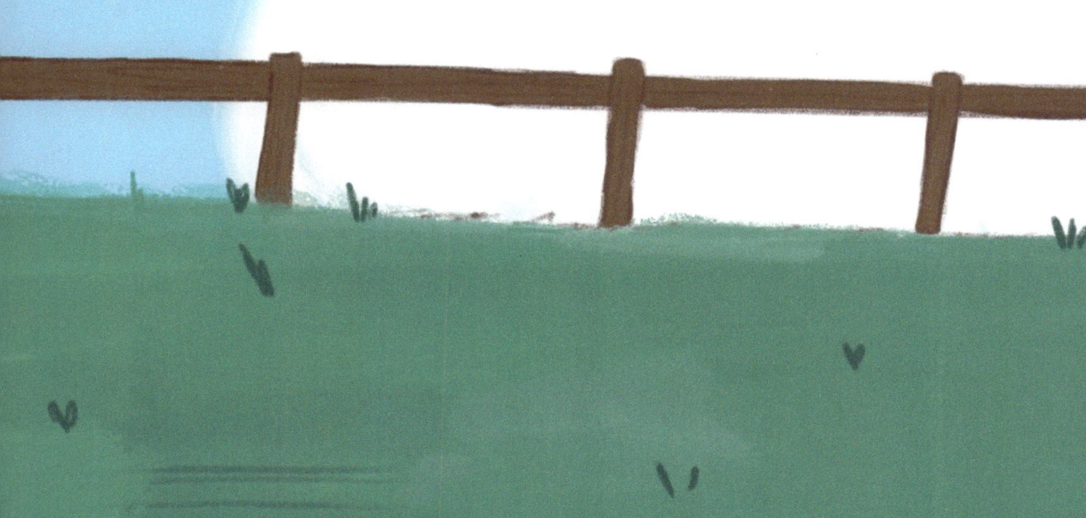

Hey there baby boy, looks like your underwater fun-time is over in there now.

No more drum-heartbeats to soothe you from mama's miracle plow.

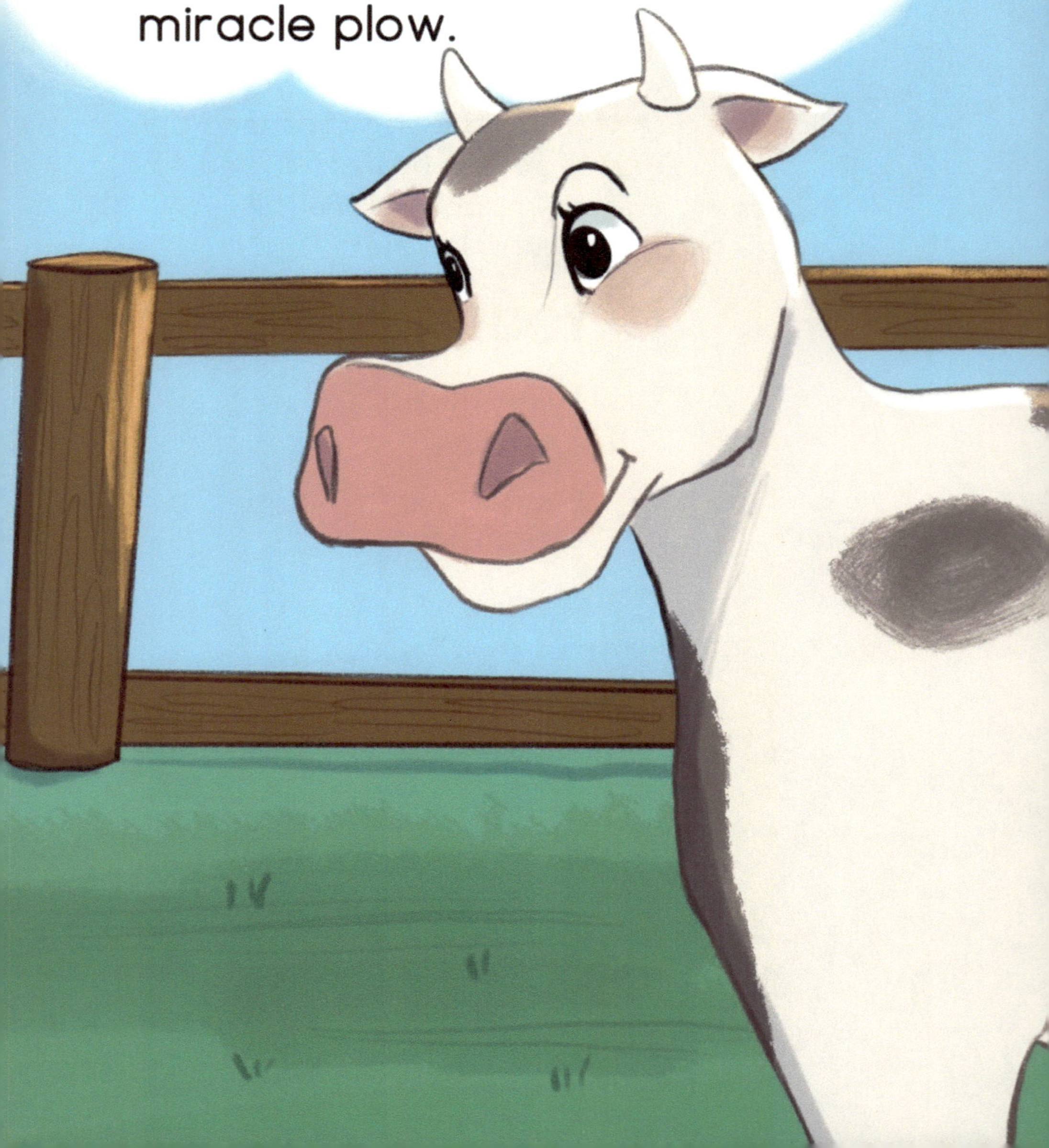

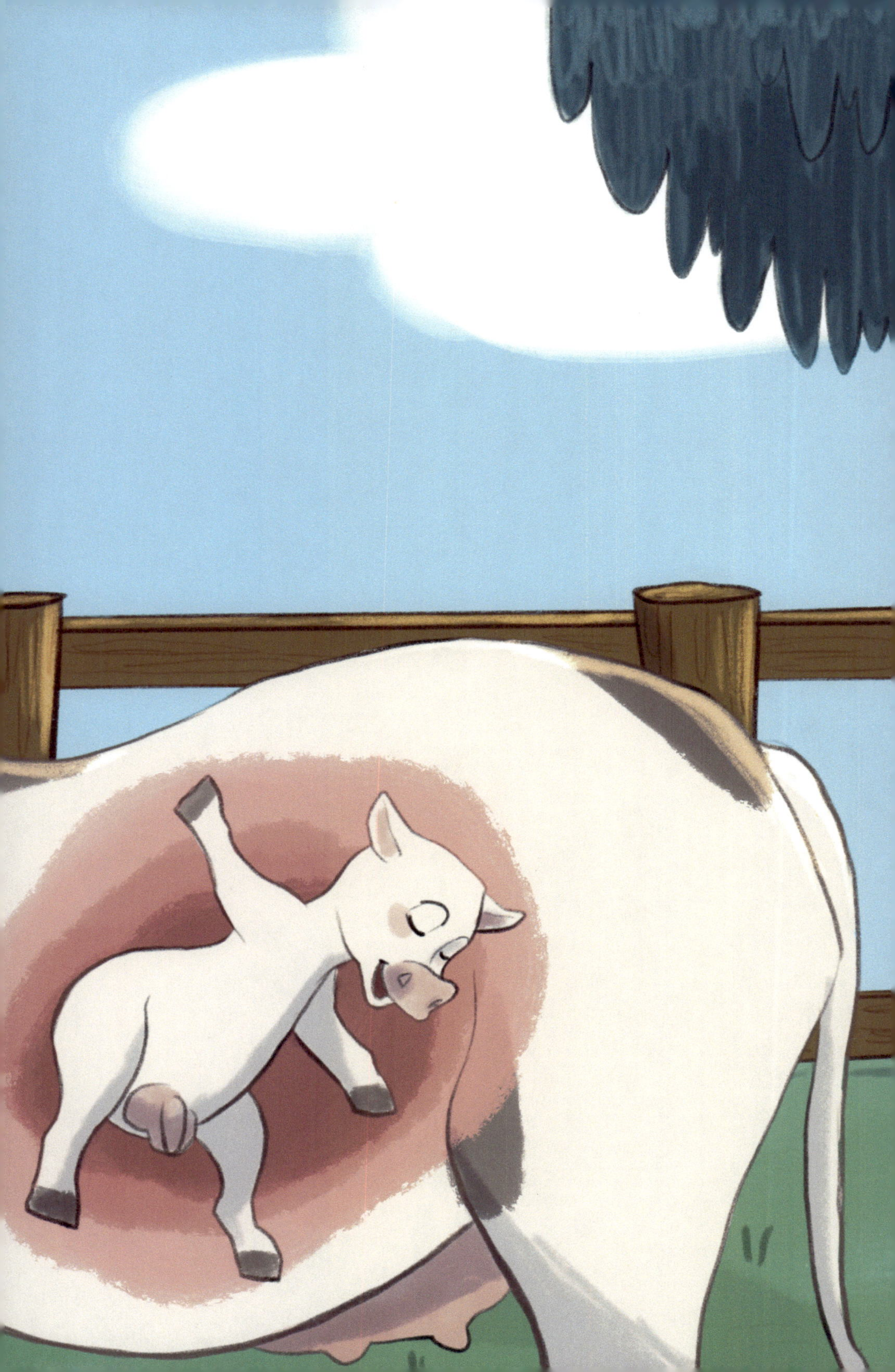

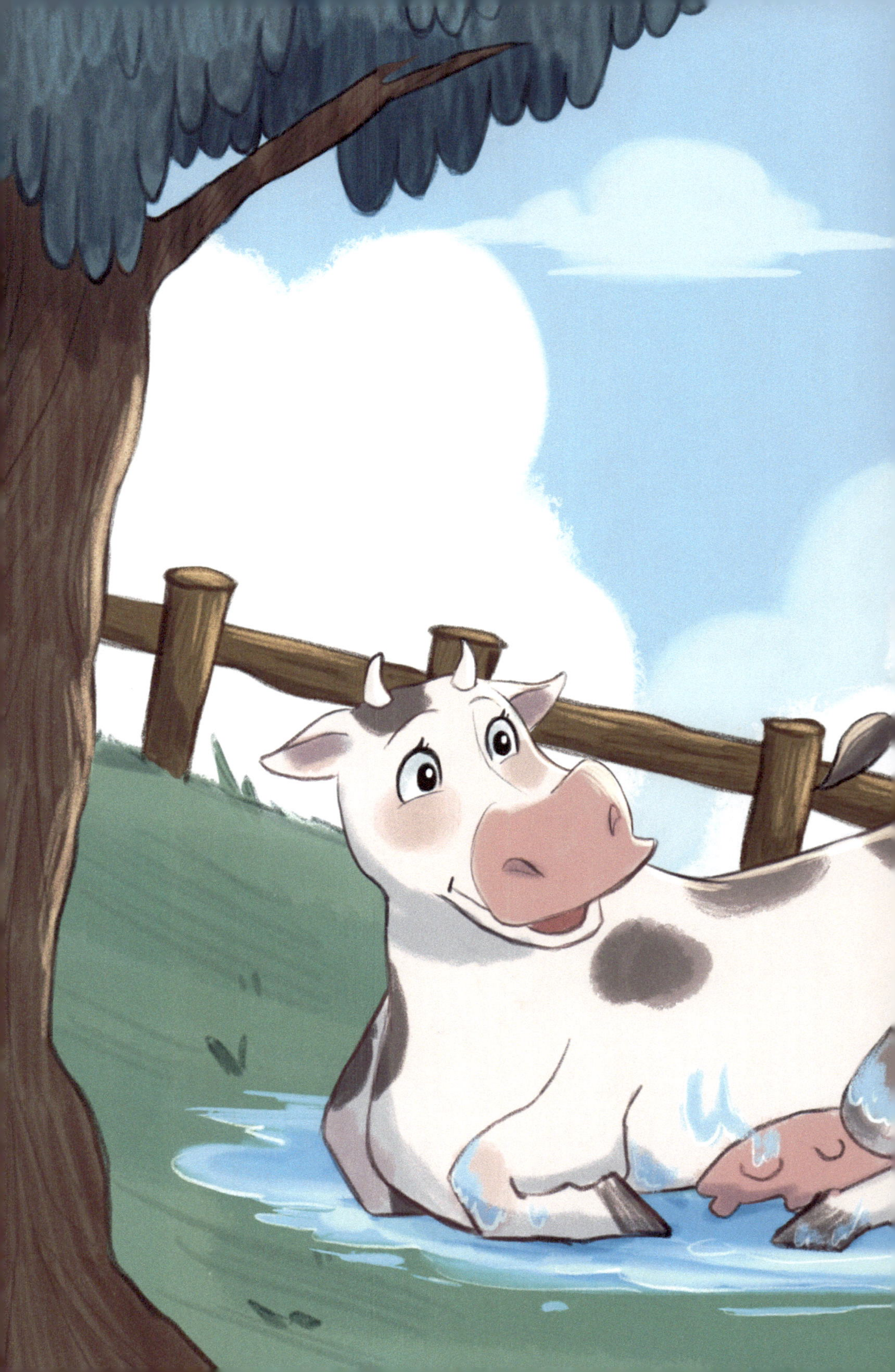

You know she didn't
sign up for her starchild
to turn into a shitty
sleepy grownup.

So, get out from that
comfortable womb
and wake the fuck up.

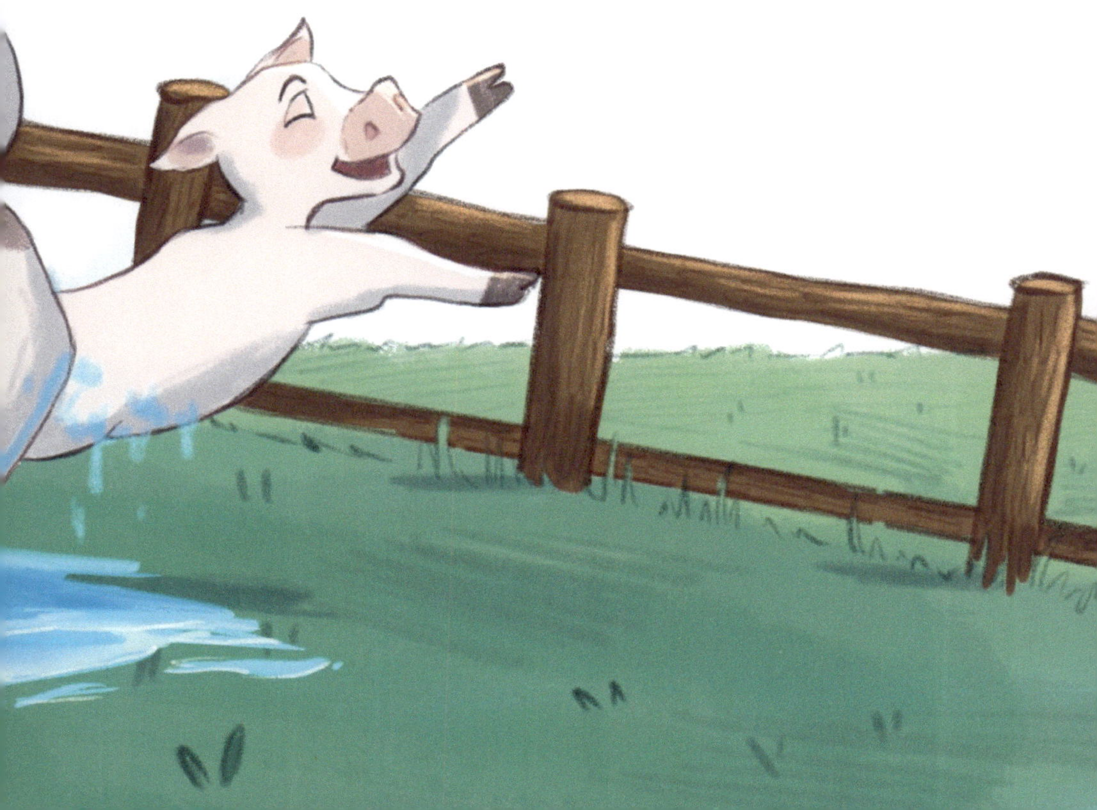

Now that you're outside of that warm Spirit world, welcome to the cold man-made one dude.

Stuck with labels and titles inside identity boxes of all sorts to get your naive ass ready to be screwed.

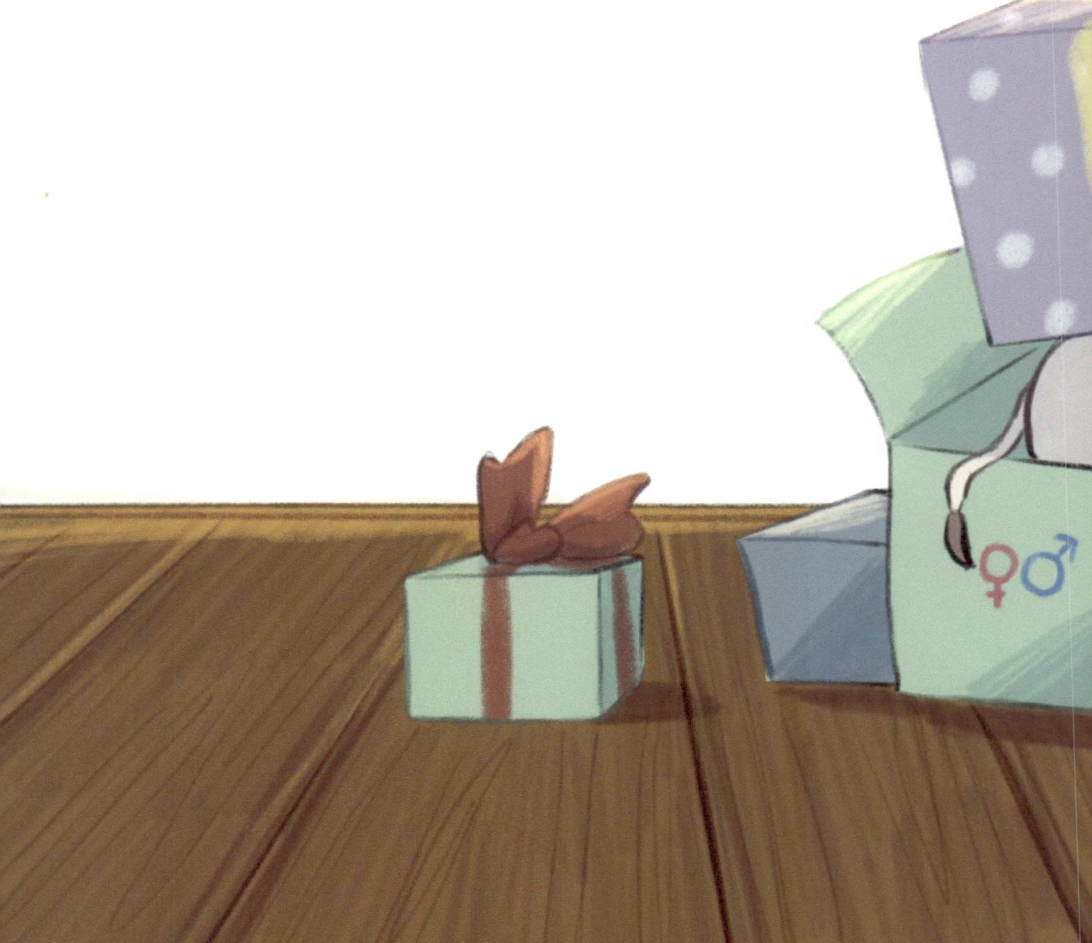

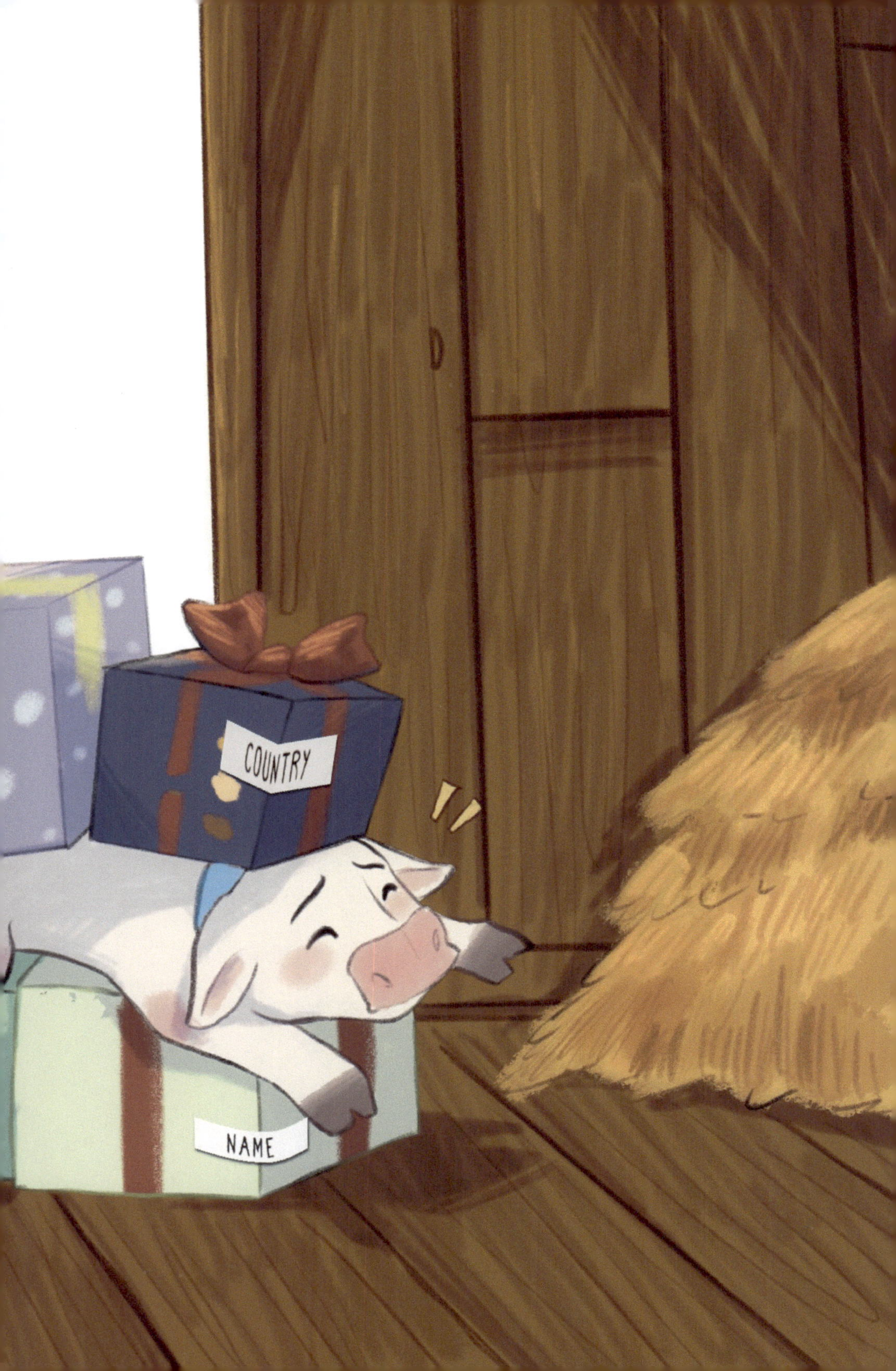
COUNTRY
NAME

The mindfuck is that you'll spend your whole life protecting and defending each of them.

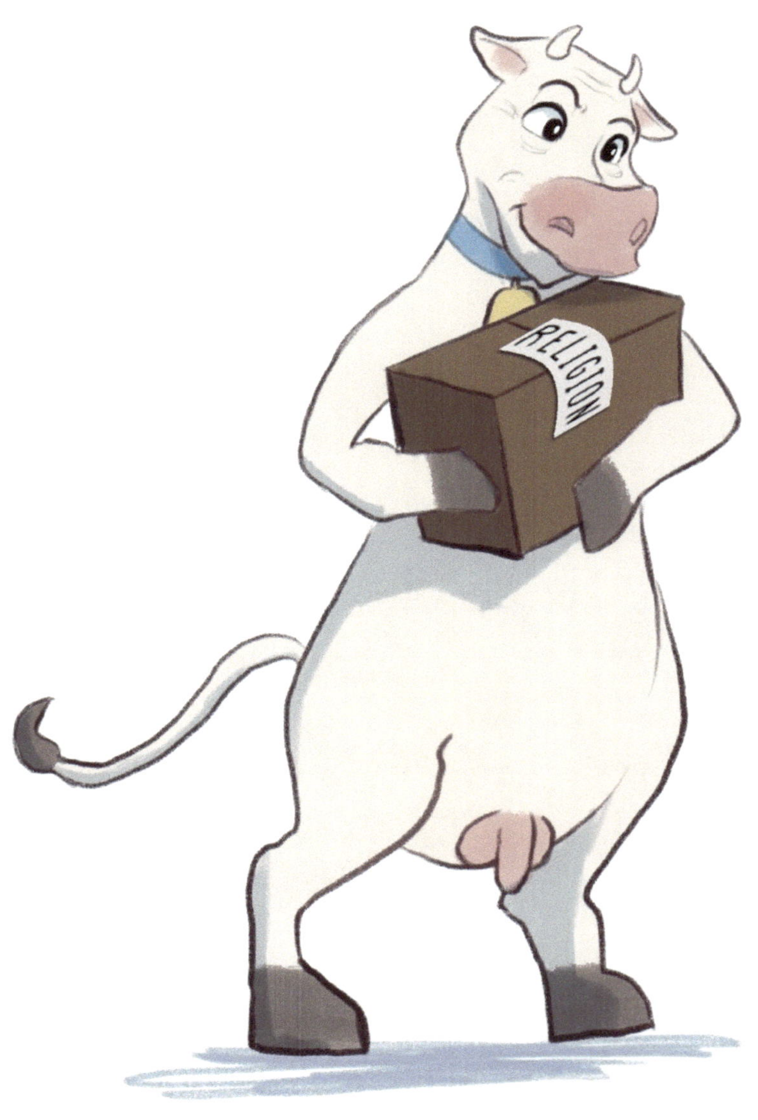

So, wake the fuck up if you want to fix any, but just don't be so quick to want to all condemn.

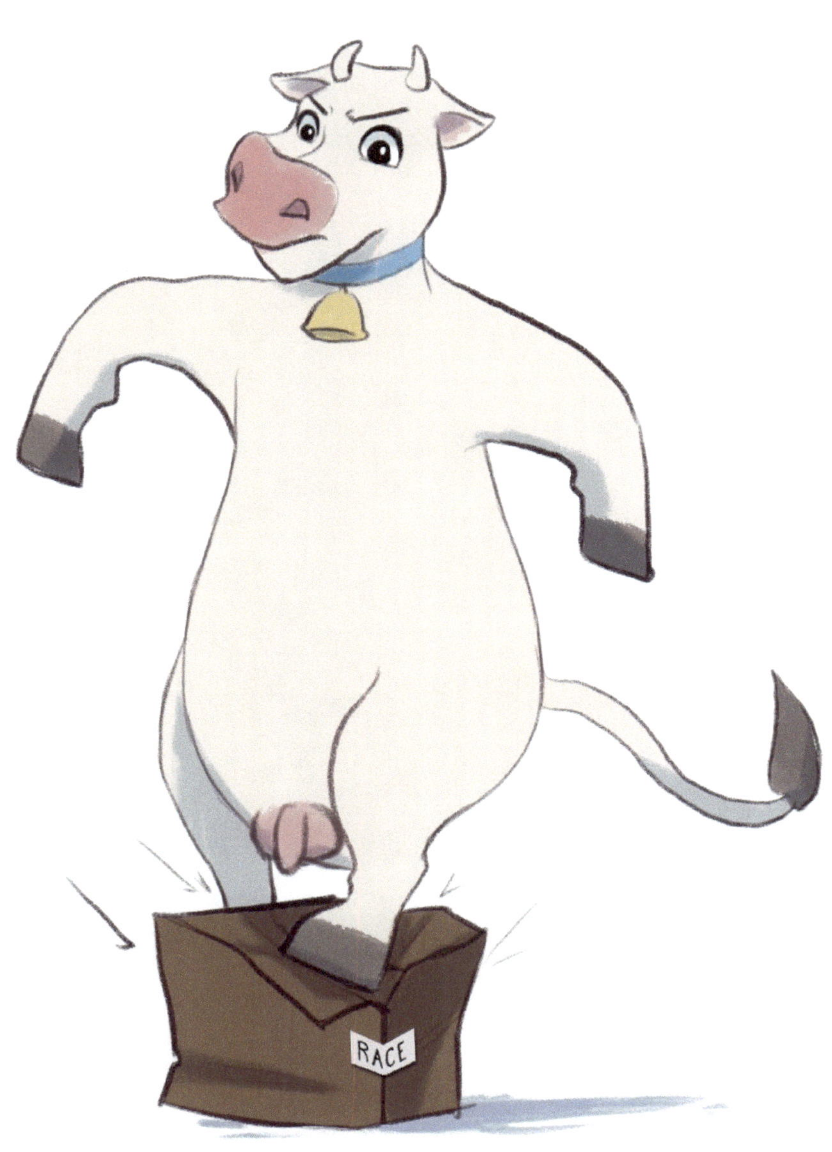

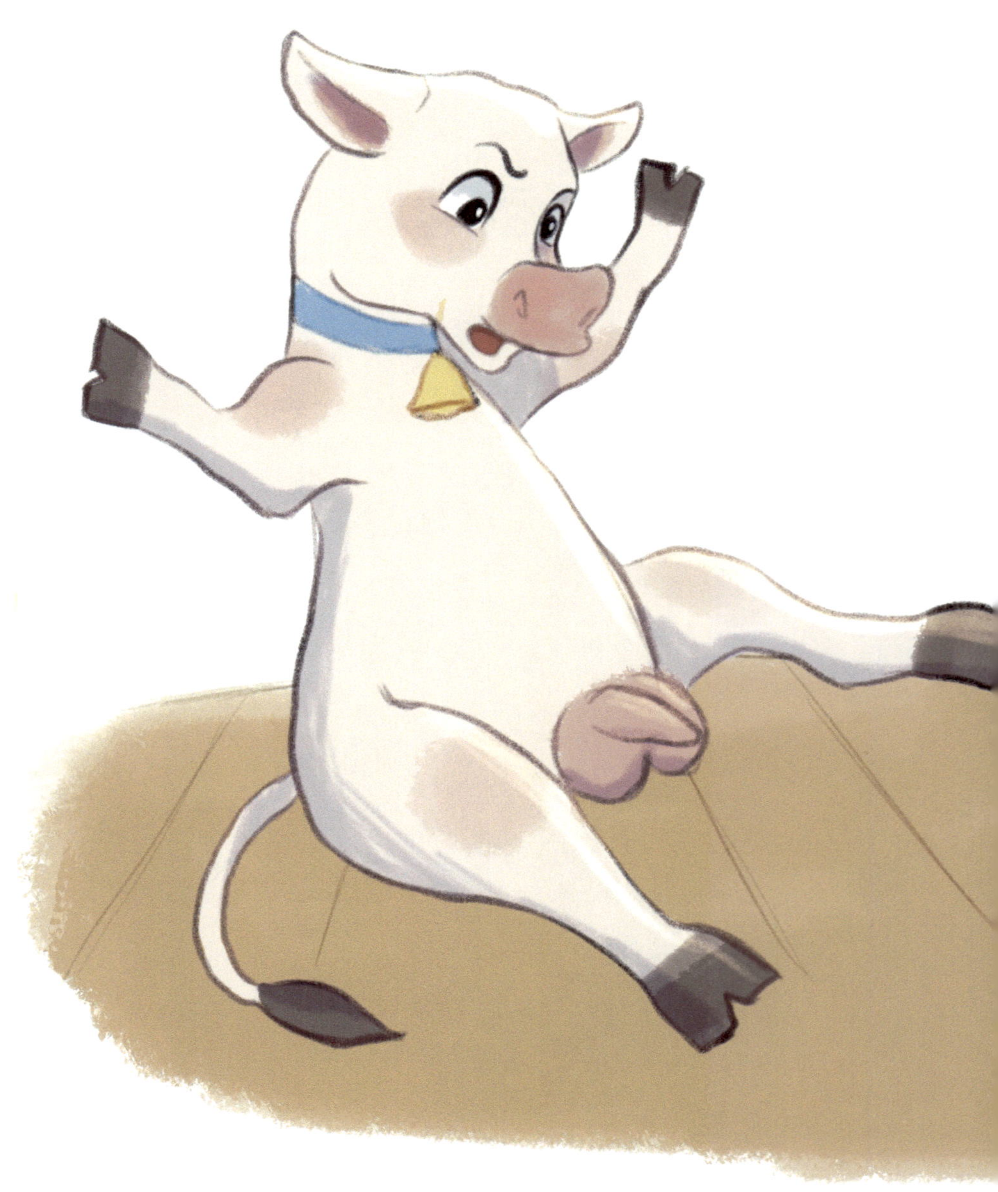

For starters, don't ask why you got that funny-looking toy on you, as it's all custom made.

Seems like your Creator flipped a coin on your ass as a joke to laugh, but not to trade.

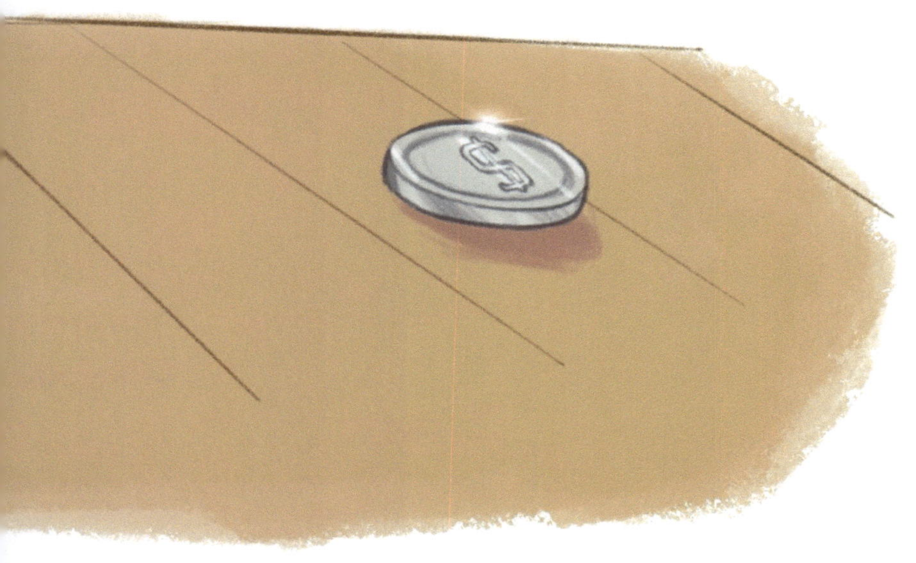

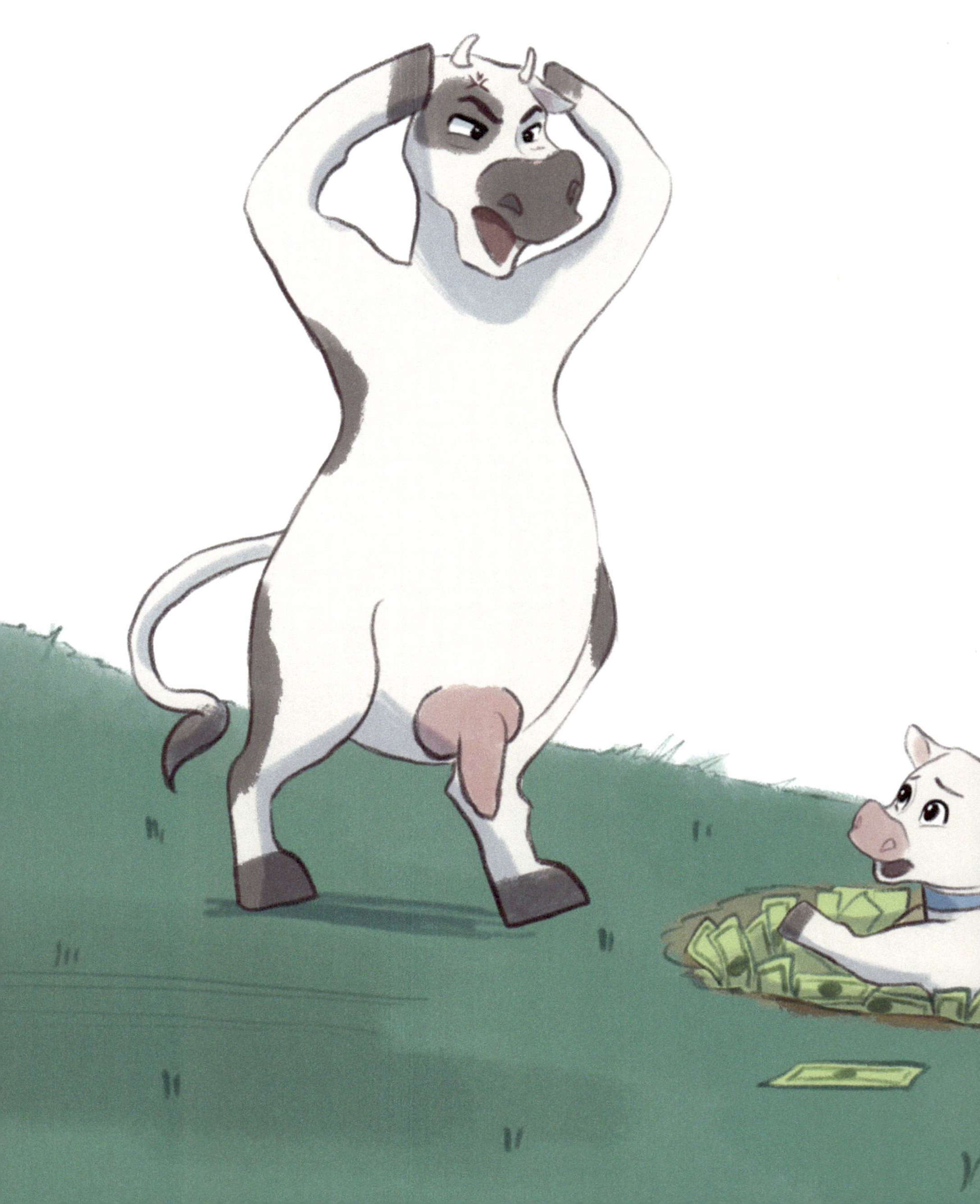

Why be so anxious to want to change any of it, or dare to ask your papa to pay for it.

It works just fine, so wake the fuck up, and try not to be a drama queen or a money pit.

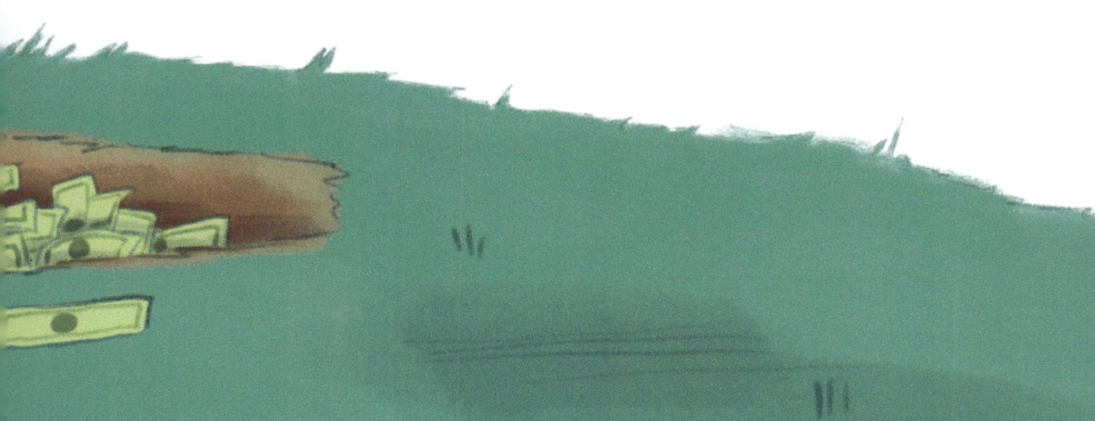

Your beauty shines from within,
so don't wear any masks
to hide, or to fit in any tribes.

If you wake the fuck up,
you'll see everyone in you
and respect all types of vibes.

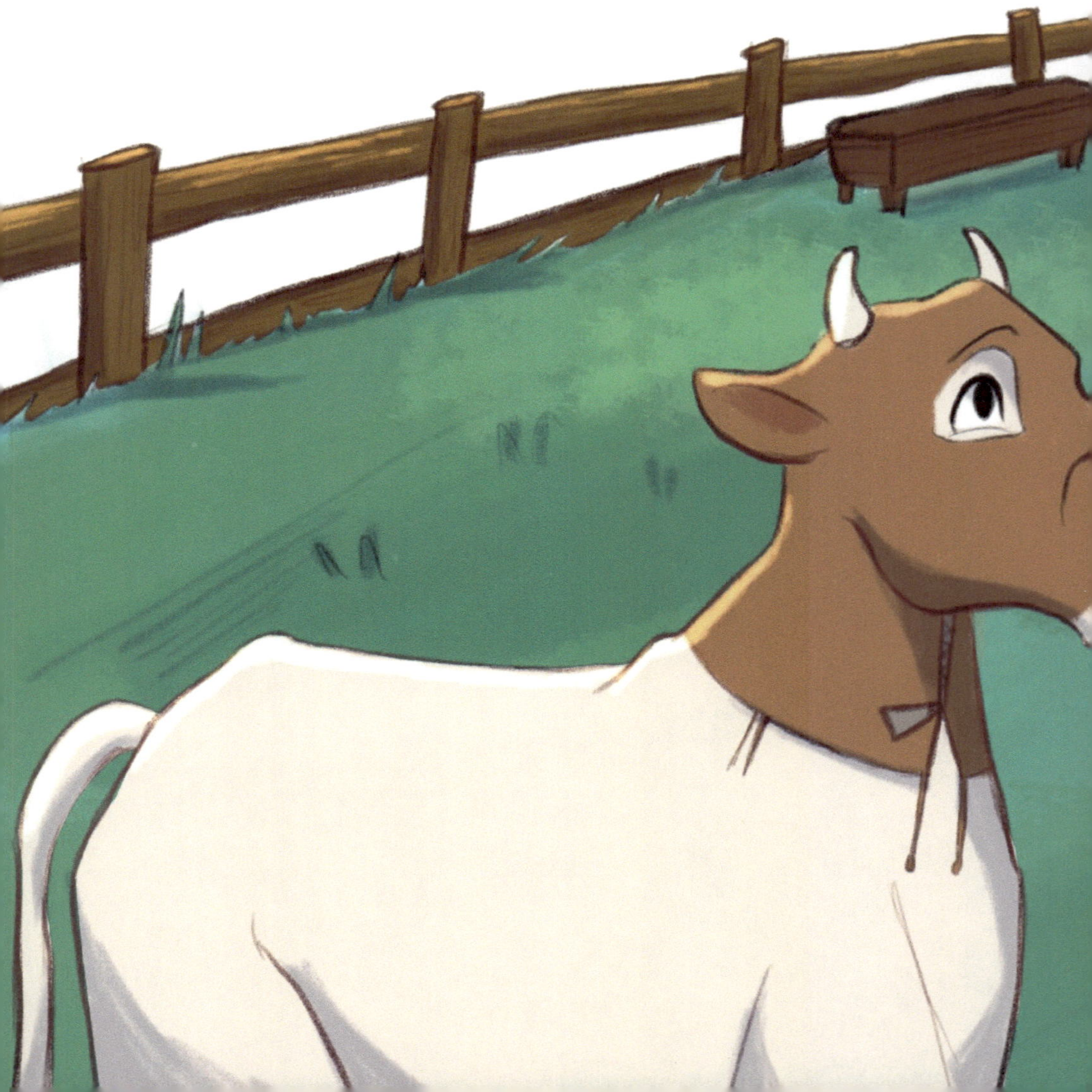

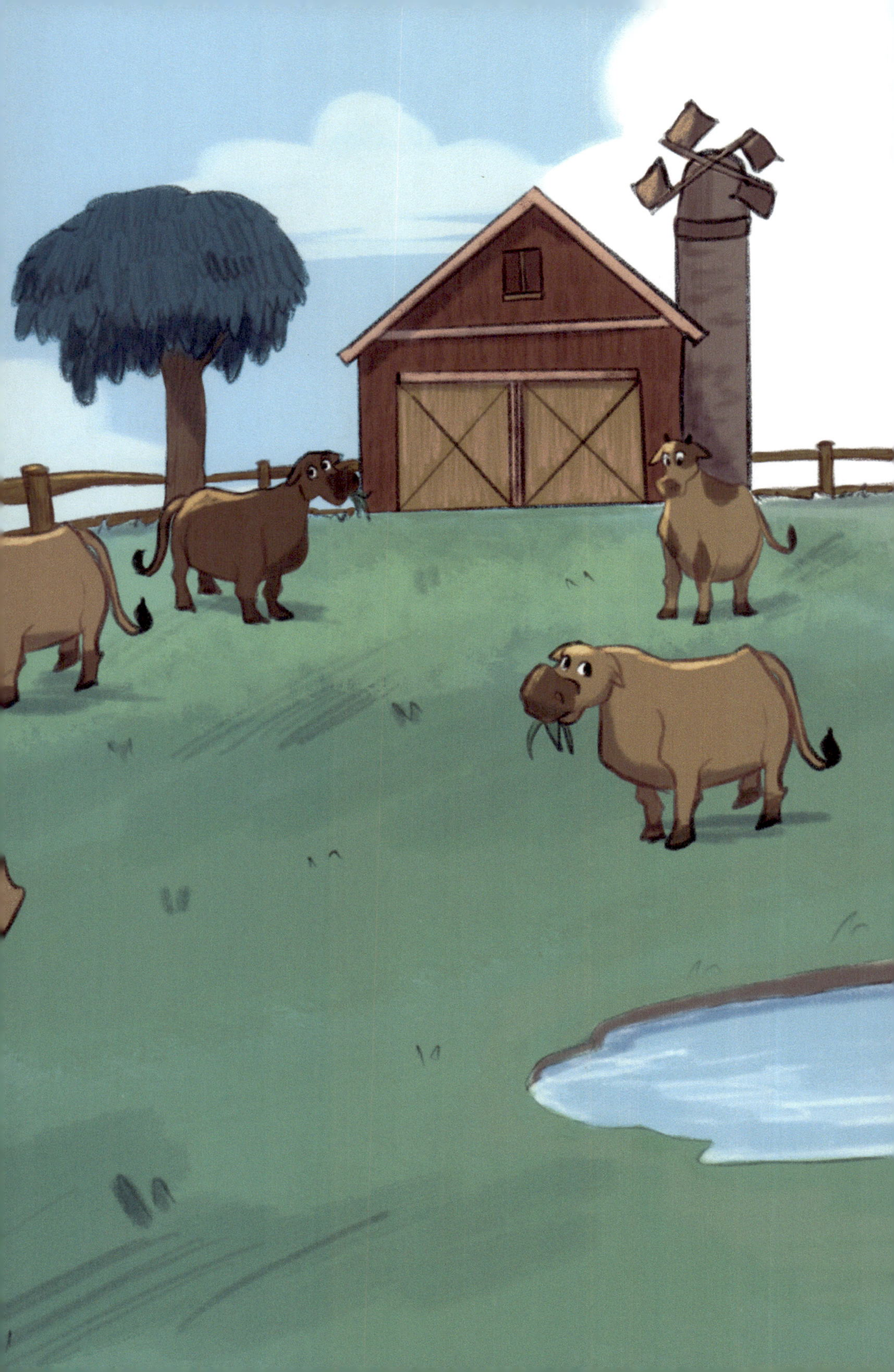

For sure, stop whining and feeling sorry for yourself as if you're a damn loser.

You raced to beat over a million sperm to want to be here as the intended user.

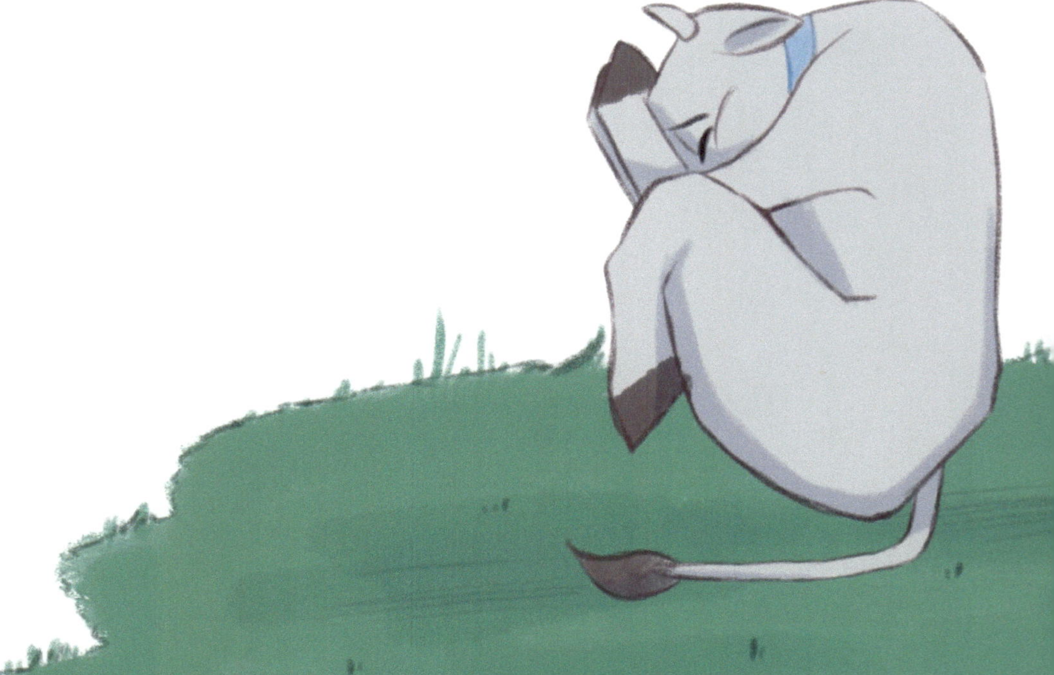

How about taking that hoof out of your mouth and raising it high like a winner.

Now get the fuck up from that fetal position, and don't wait for a human to eat you for dinner.

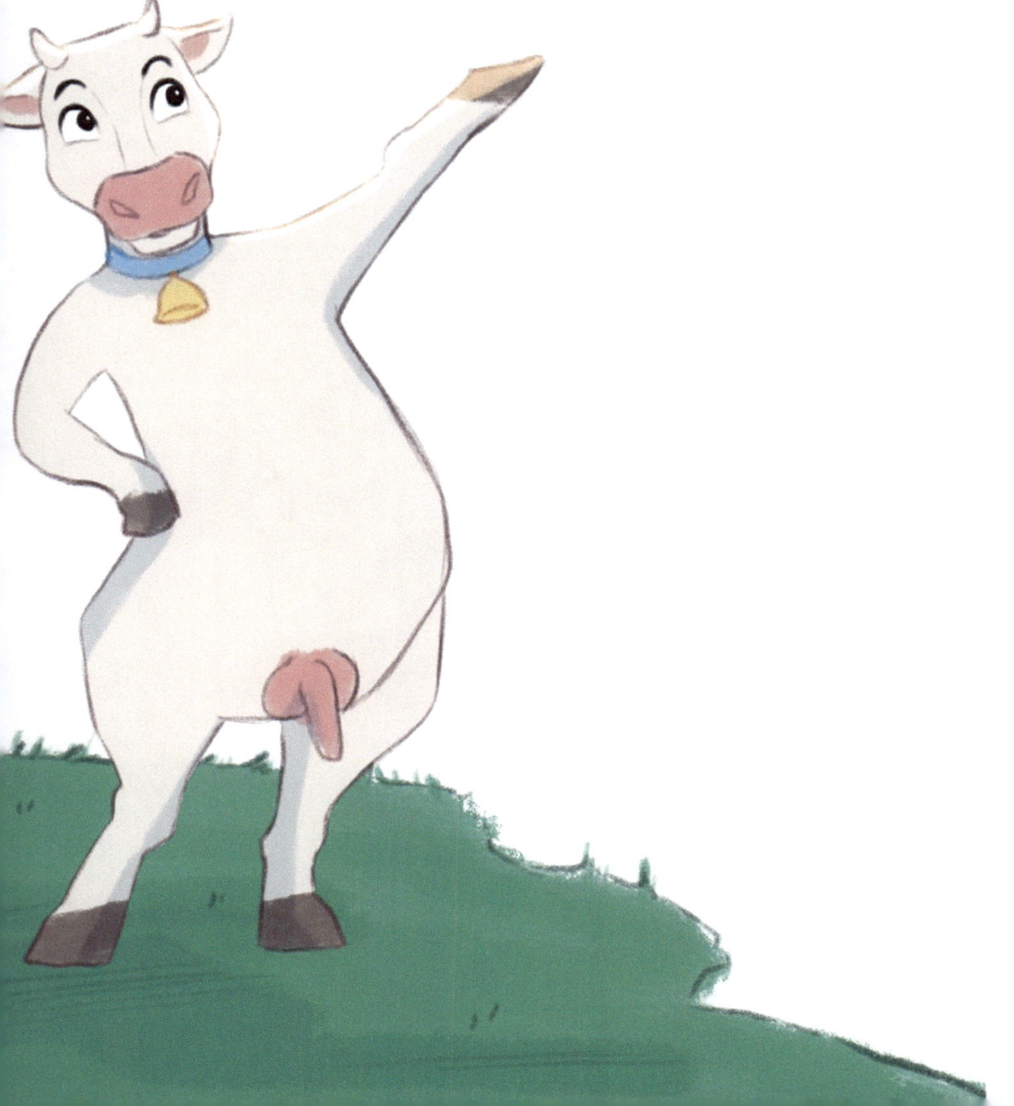

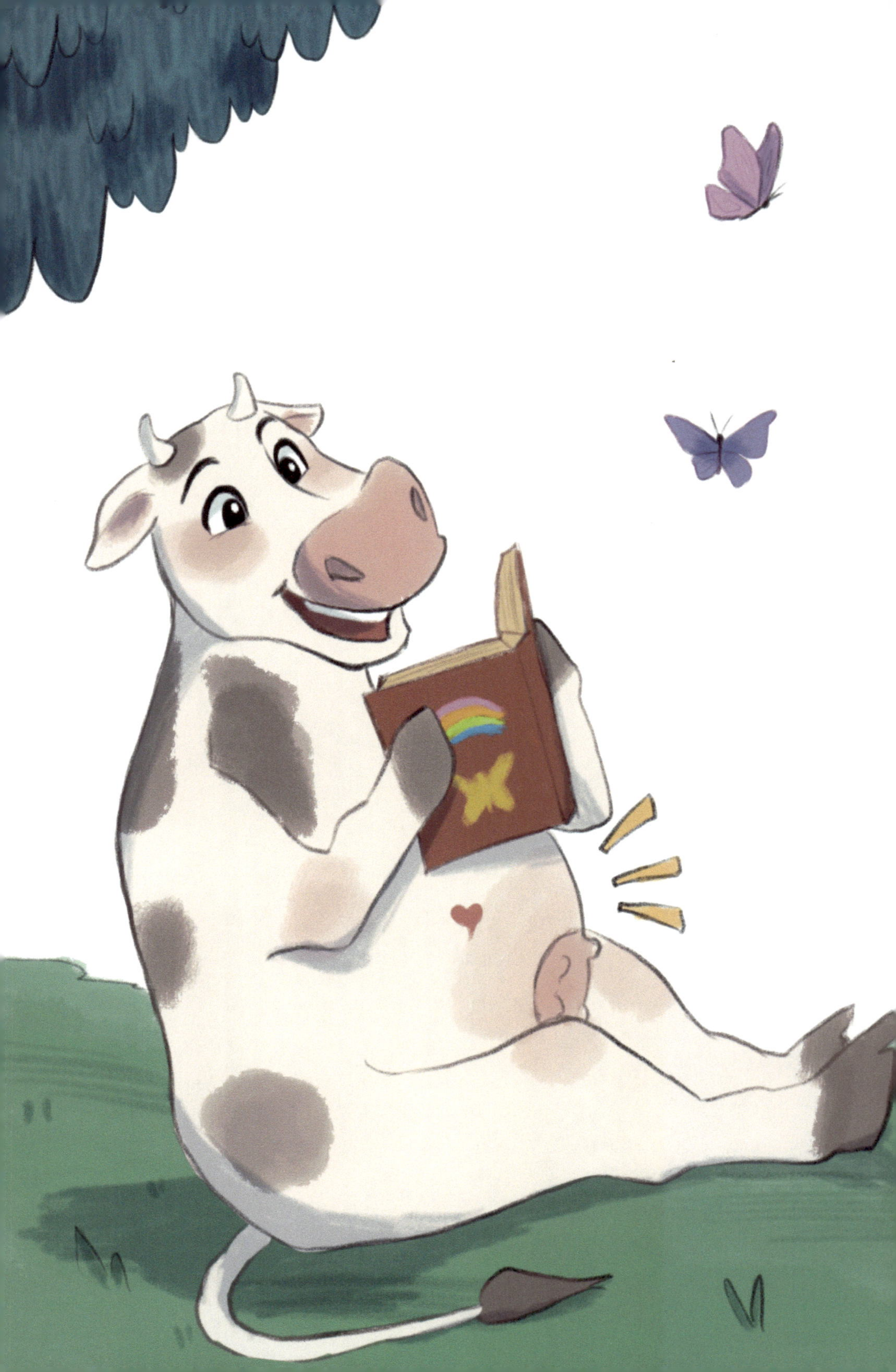

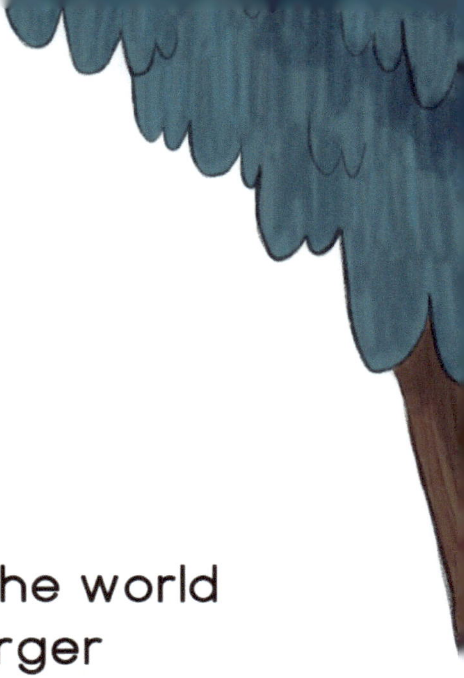

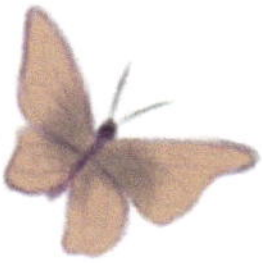

You can pretend the world outside is just a larger version of the one you left.

Perhaps your mama read you too many fairy tales, not preparing you for any bereft.

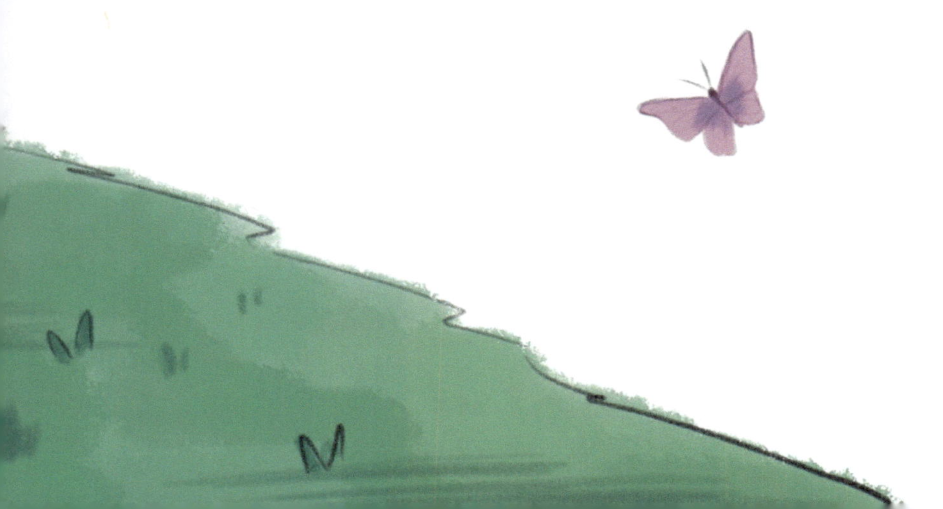

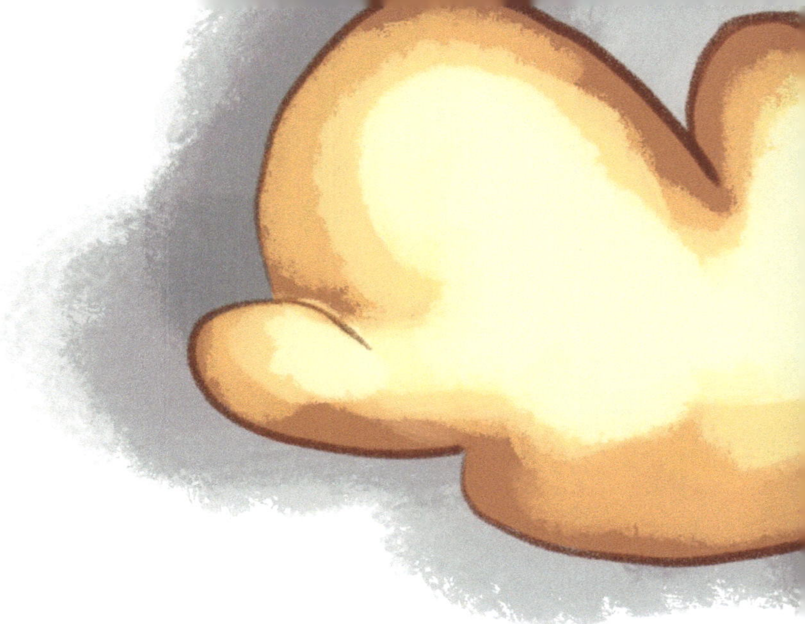

But there were good reasons why you were crying when you got out of her.

Yep, this is a wild and crazy place, so wake the fuck up and don't be a warmonger.

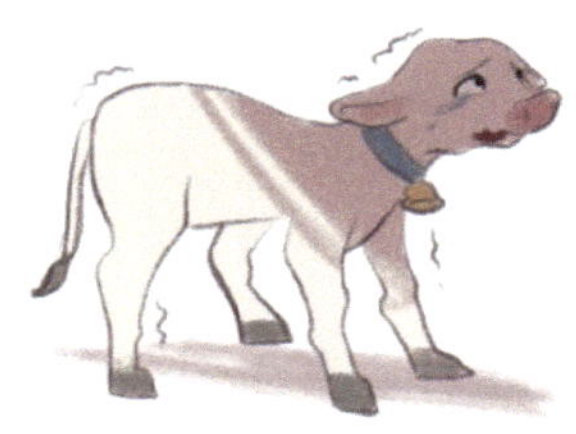

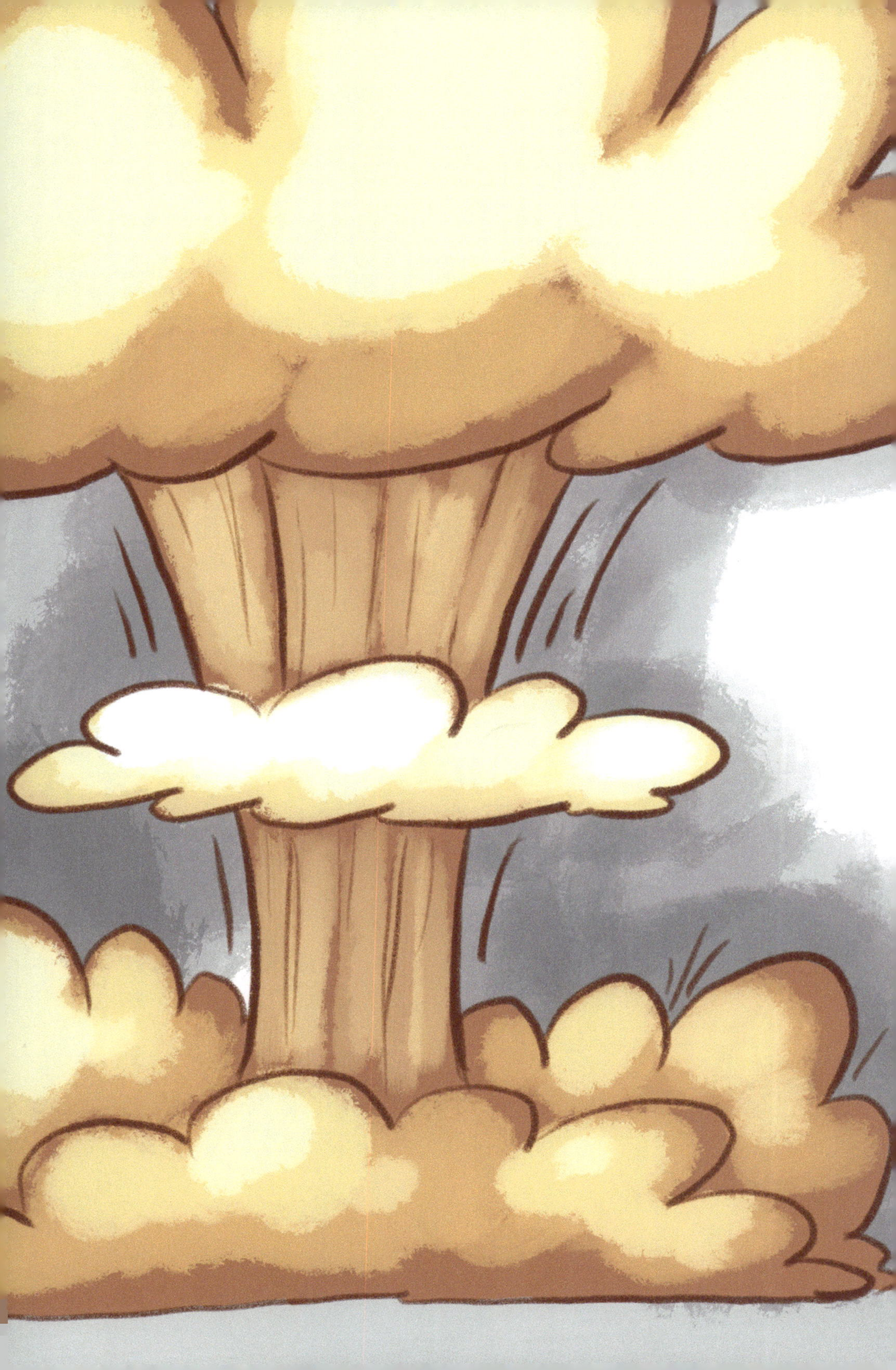

This round floating planet you chose to visit in your mortal vessel is a bonafide mess.

Millions of years here, and it's still turning despite being corrupted by human excess.

As are the smiling faces greeting you, who look as fake as vegan milk for you to caress.

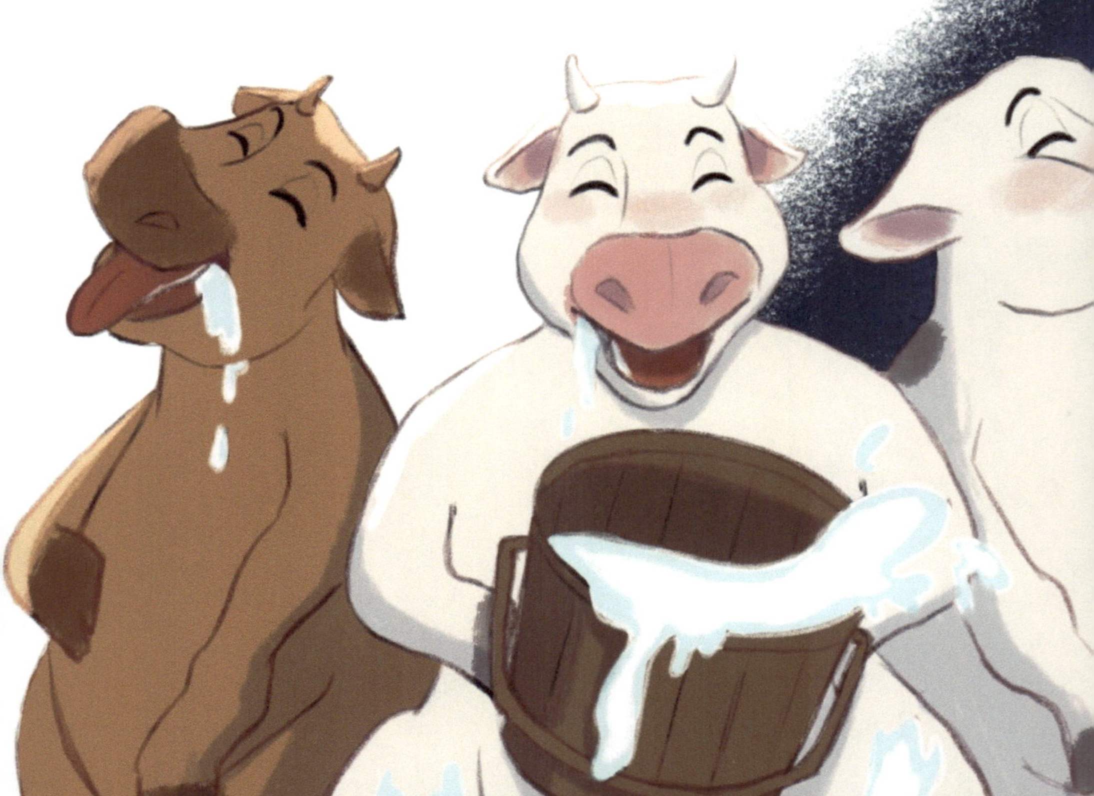

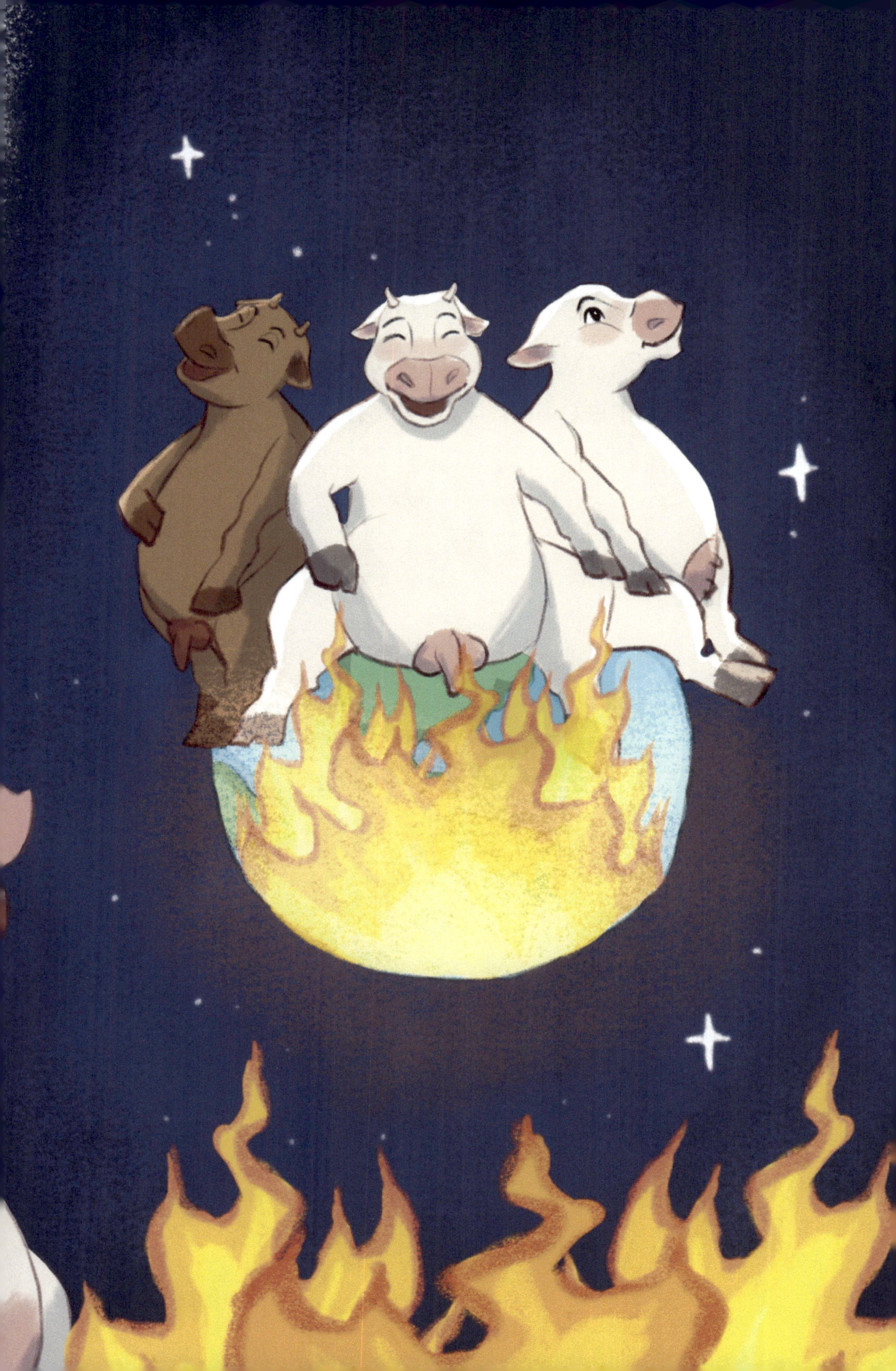

These grownups are your anointed elders, protectors and mostly idiots in charge.

They think they know what's good for you, only to turn you into a greater fool at large.

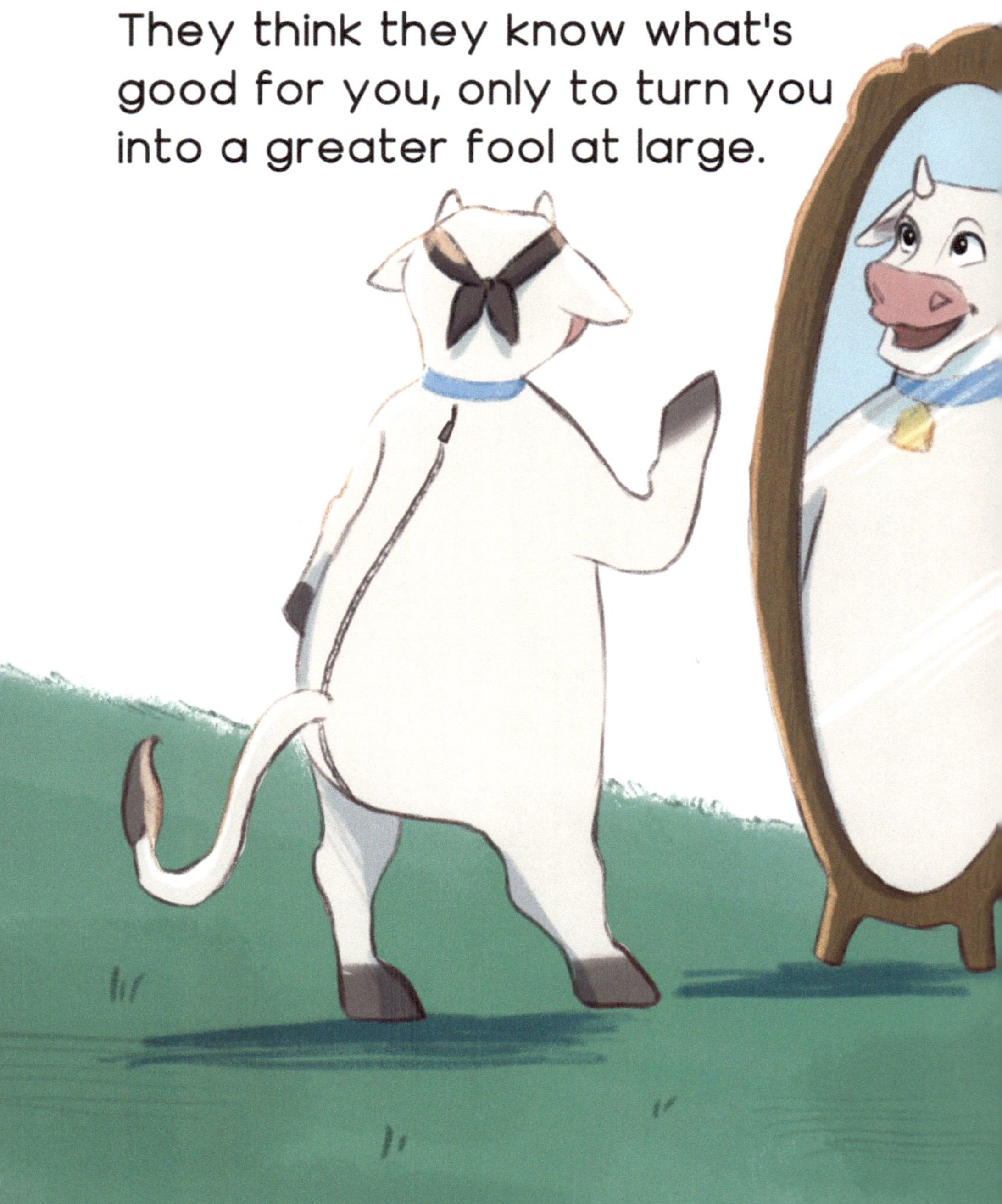

By conforming to their egoic and selfish ways, your mirror of truth is deceiving you.

What the fuck man, you best wake up or you too will be blindfolded and be so untrue.

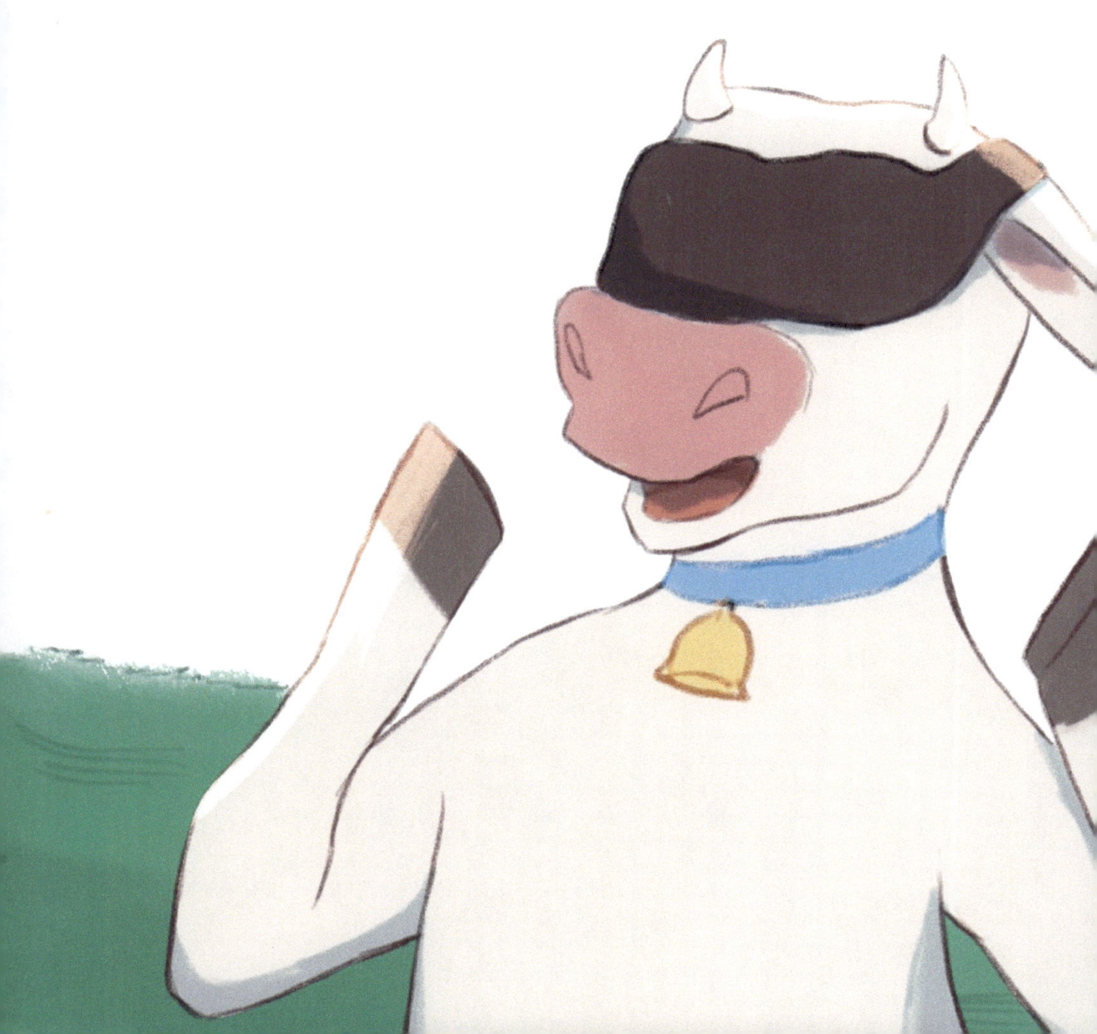

For thousands of years, these adults have evolved to be so wise they say.

Too bad their misguided ways have not always kept them from going astray.

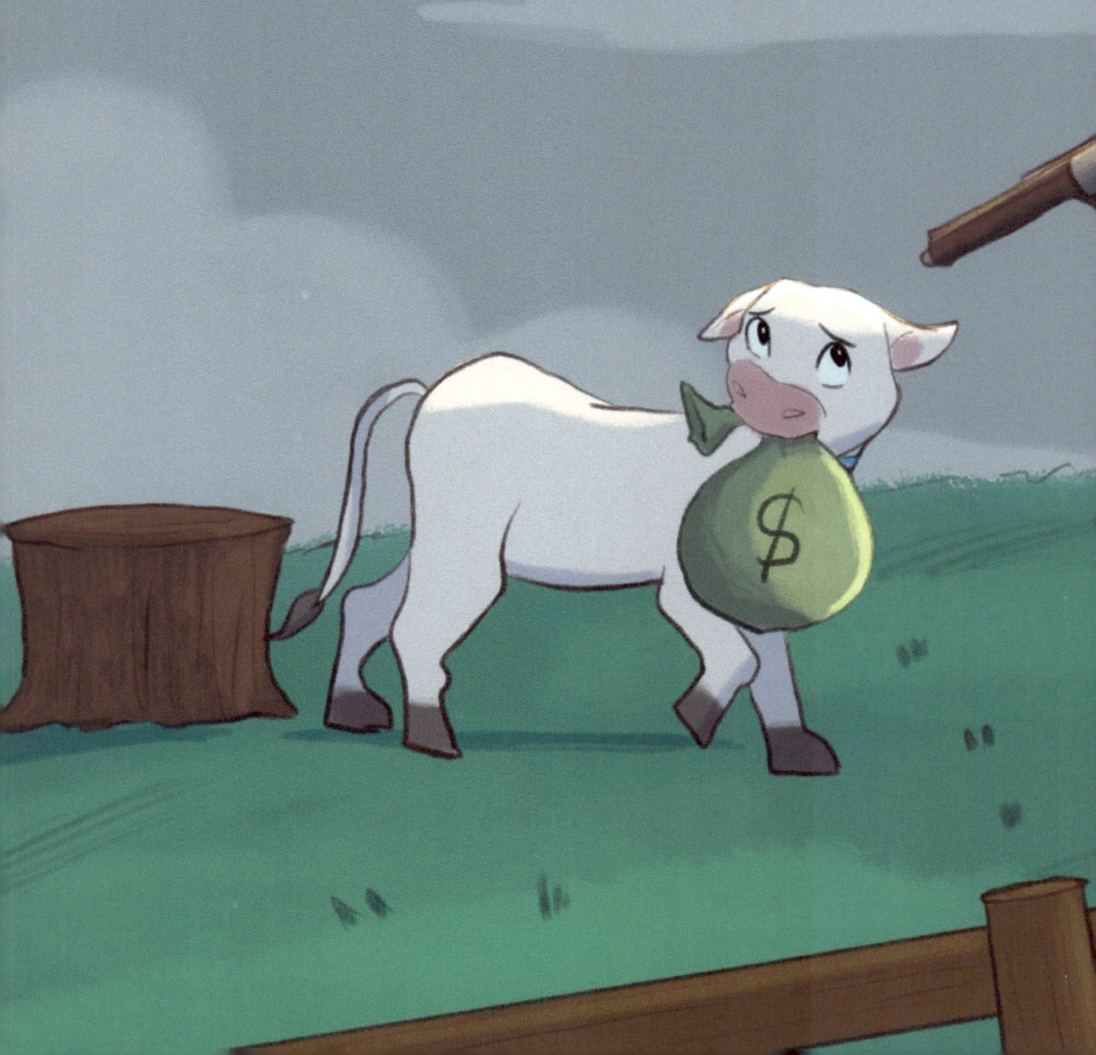

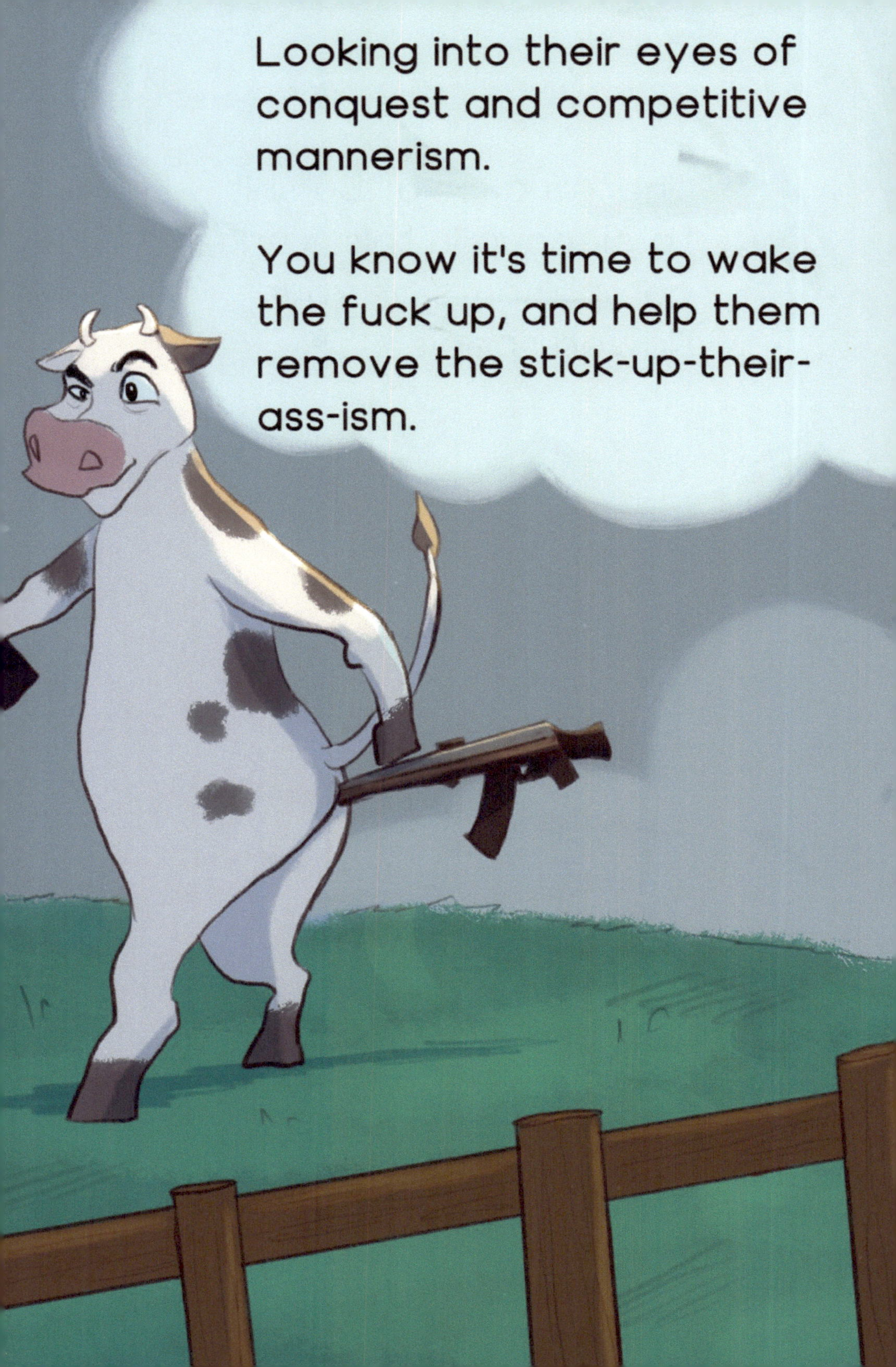
Looking into their eyes of conquest and competitive mannerism.
You know it's time to wake the fuck up, and help them remove the stick-up-their-ass-ism.

There's a lot of bullshit to cleanup in this world, compliments of your flawed species.

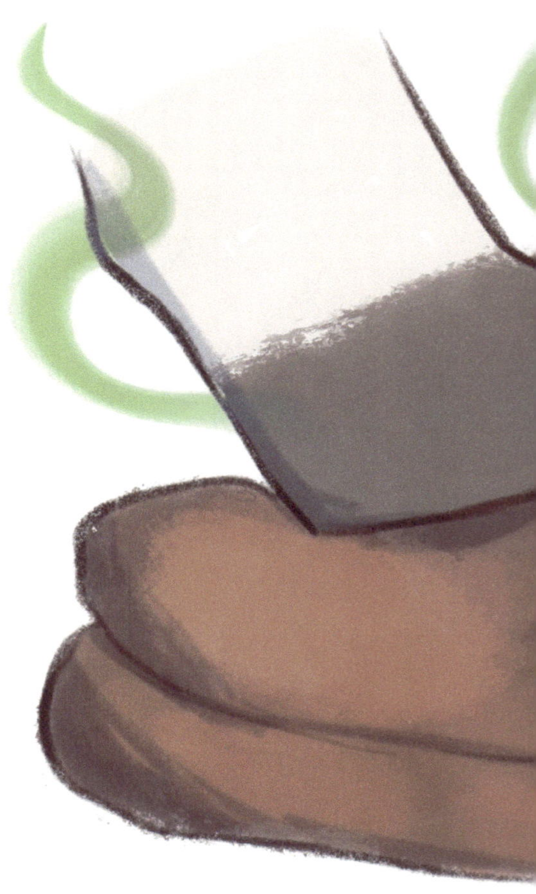

The same life form that gave birth to you, treats its own kind like animals made of feces.

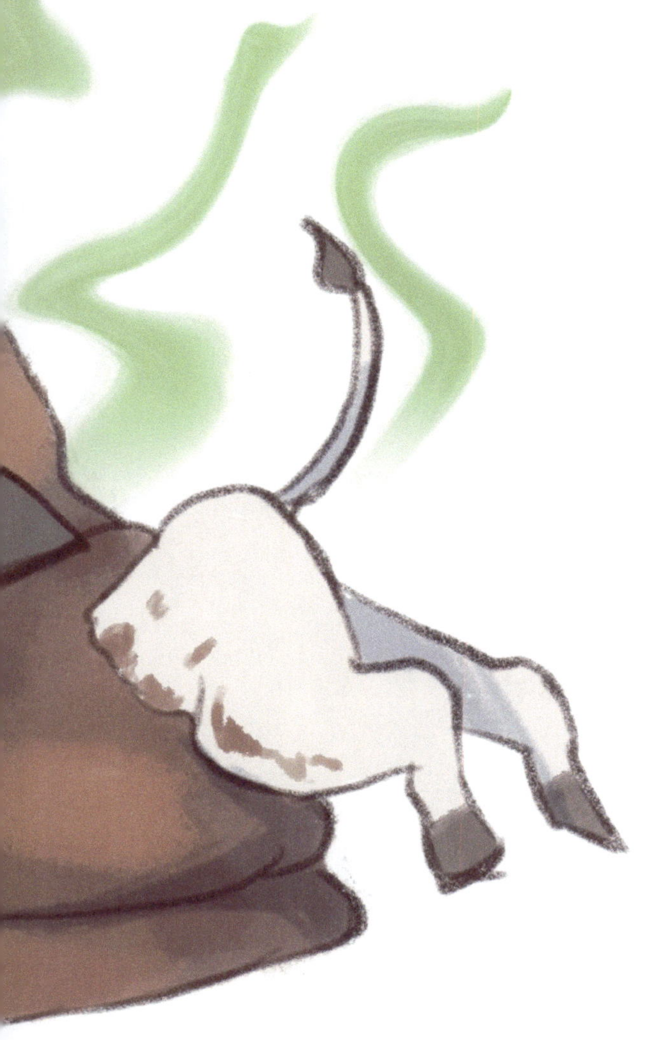

As the hungry wolves love to milk you, the feeble turn into sheeple walking blindly in a backwards direction.

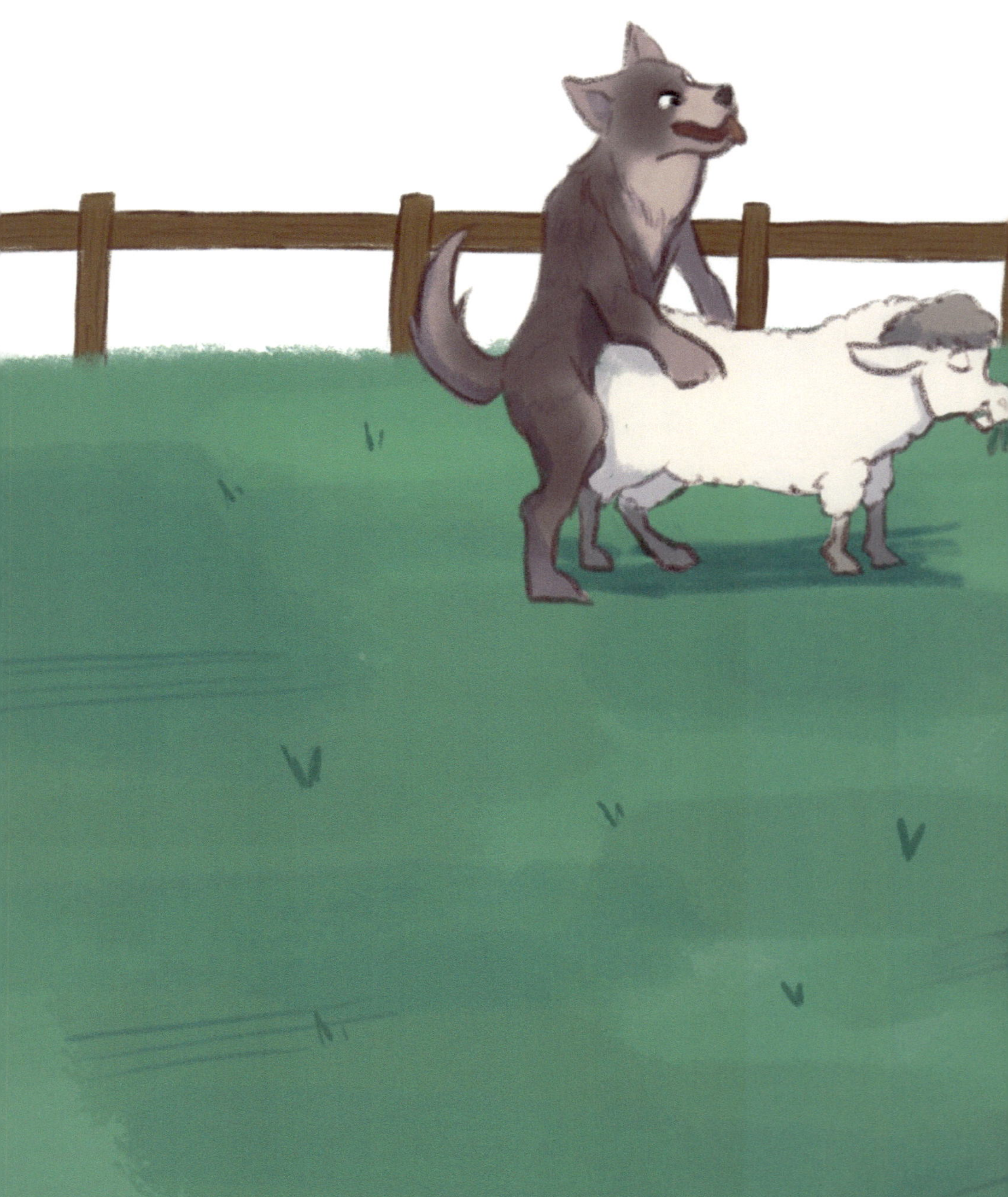

Say, what if you wake the fuck up and jerk off your stress with some straight shooting ejaculation?

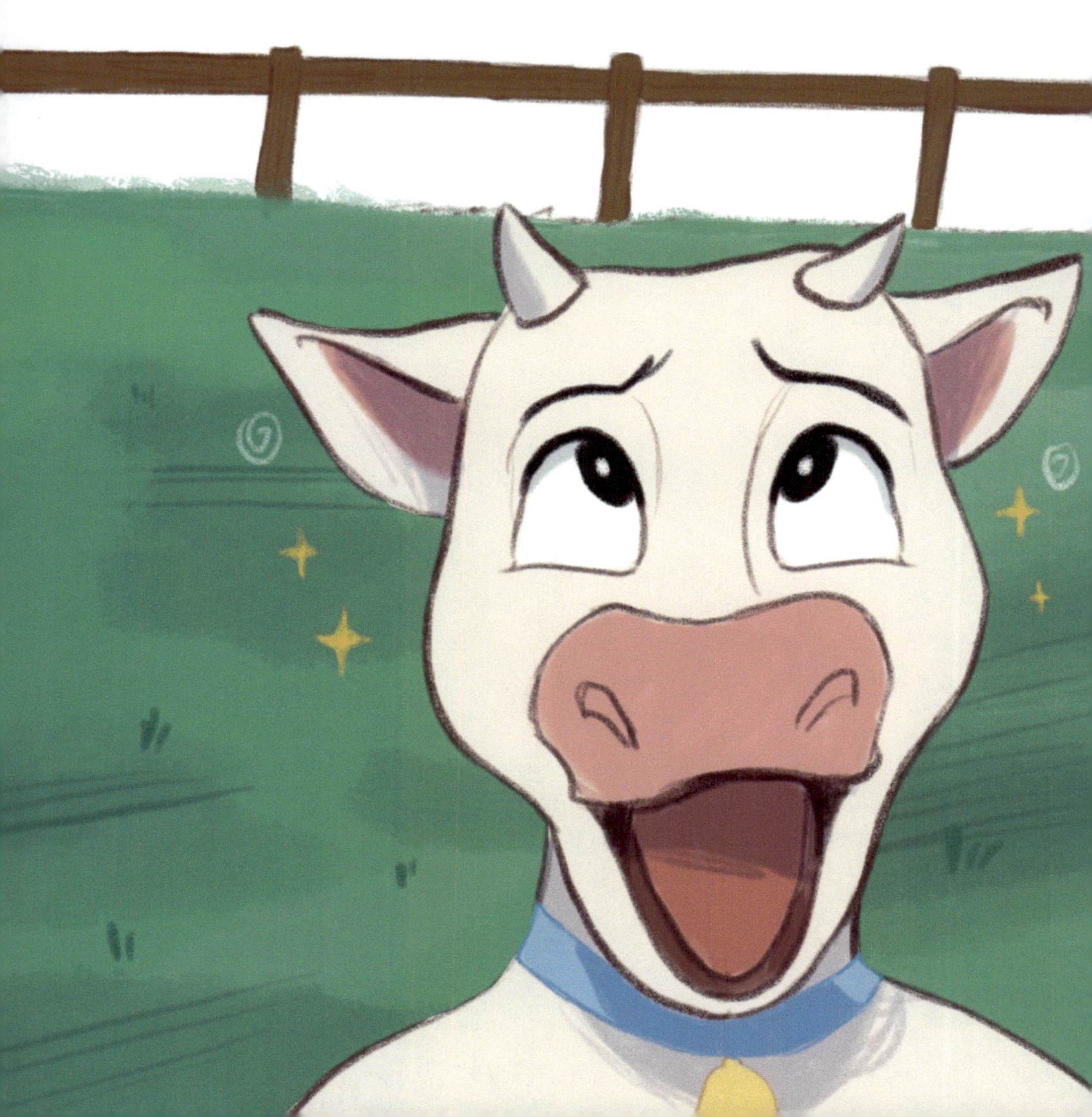

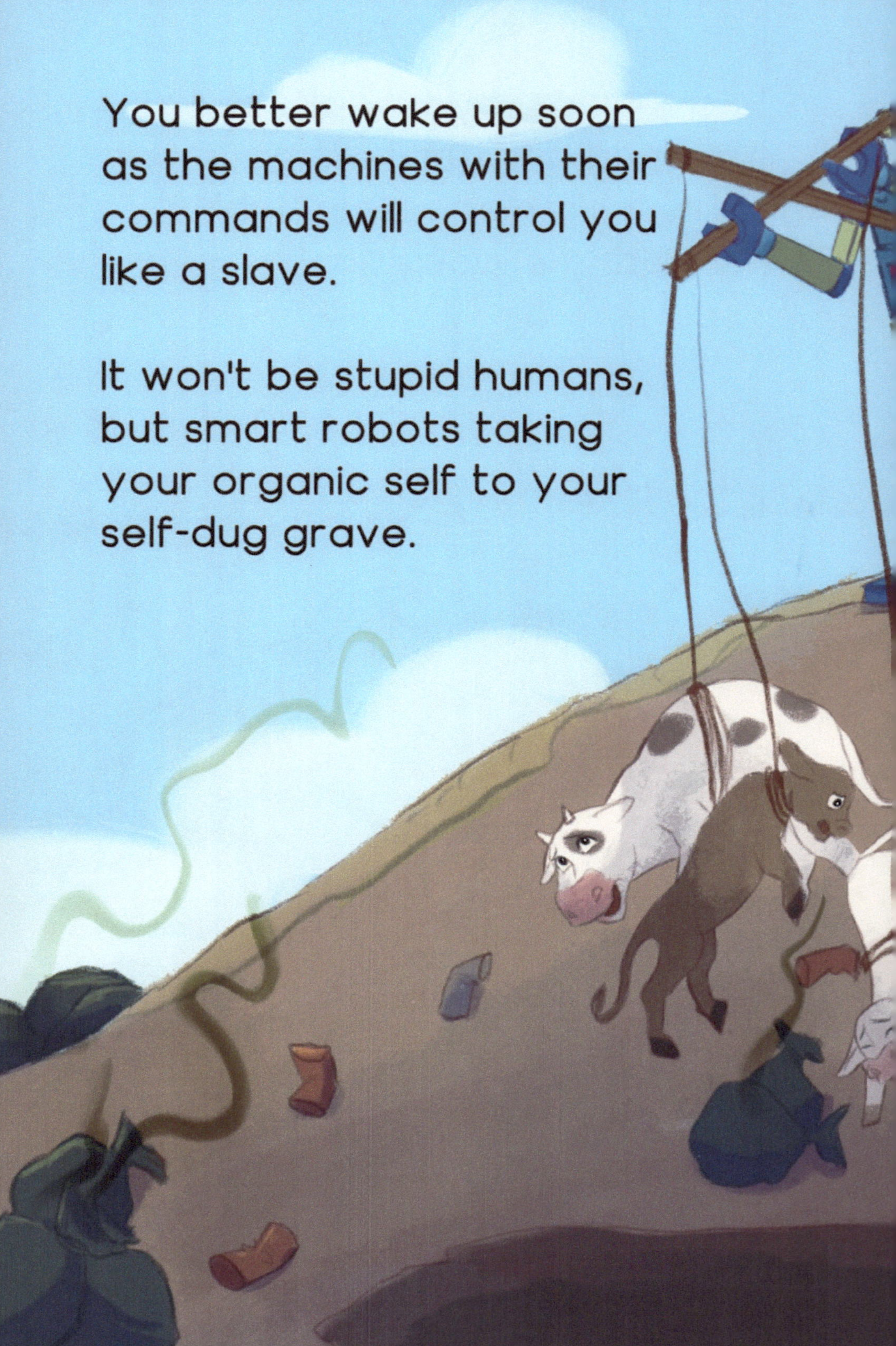

You better wake up soon as the machines with their commands will control you like a slave.

It won't be stupid humans, but smart robots taking your organic self to your self-dug grave.

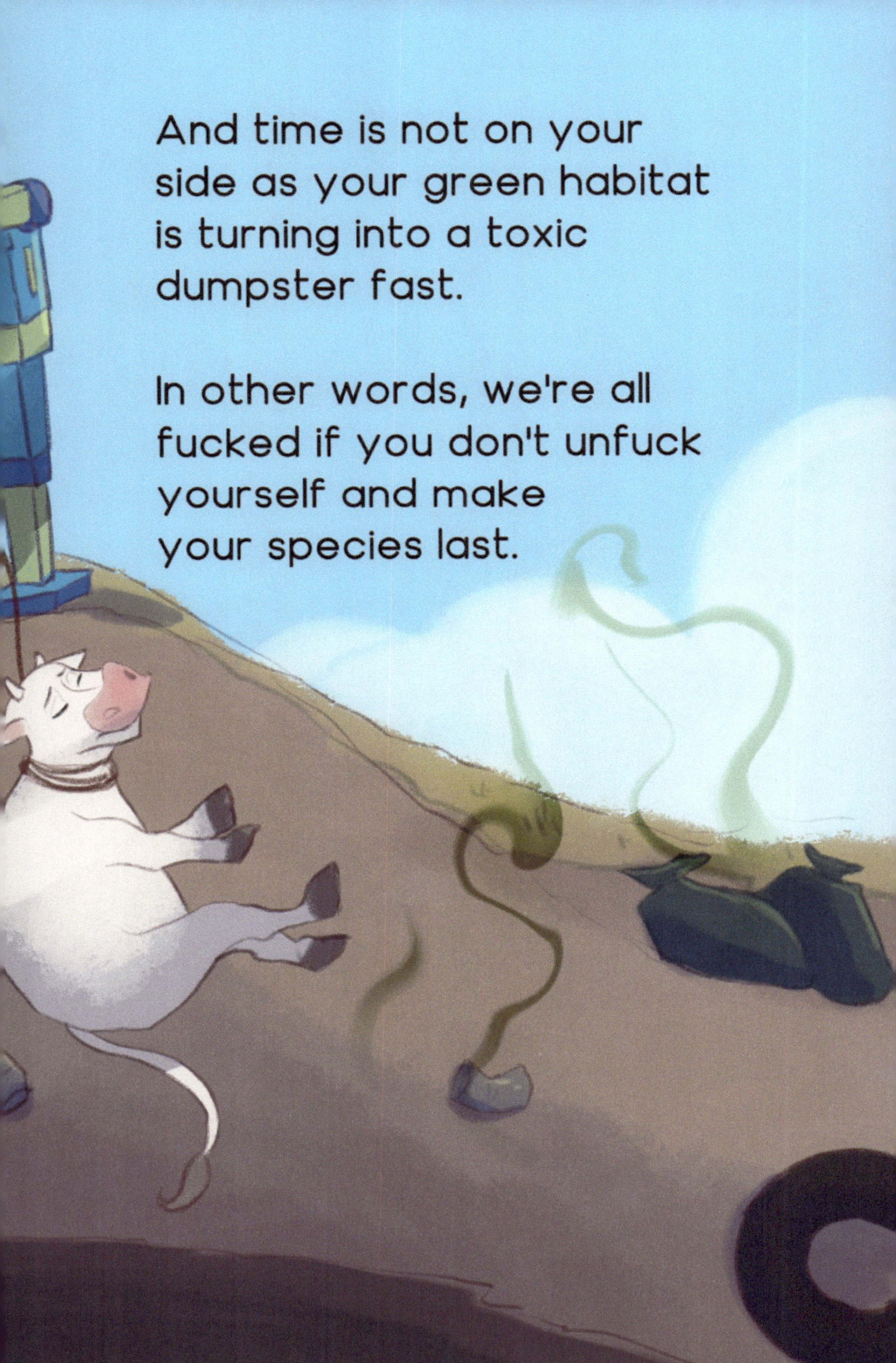

And time is not on your side as your green habitat is turning into a toxic dumpster fast.

In other words, we're all fucked if you don't unfuck yourself and make your species last.

For sure, don't count on any holy beliefs in this herd-mentality life to enlighten, or save you.

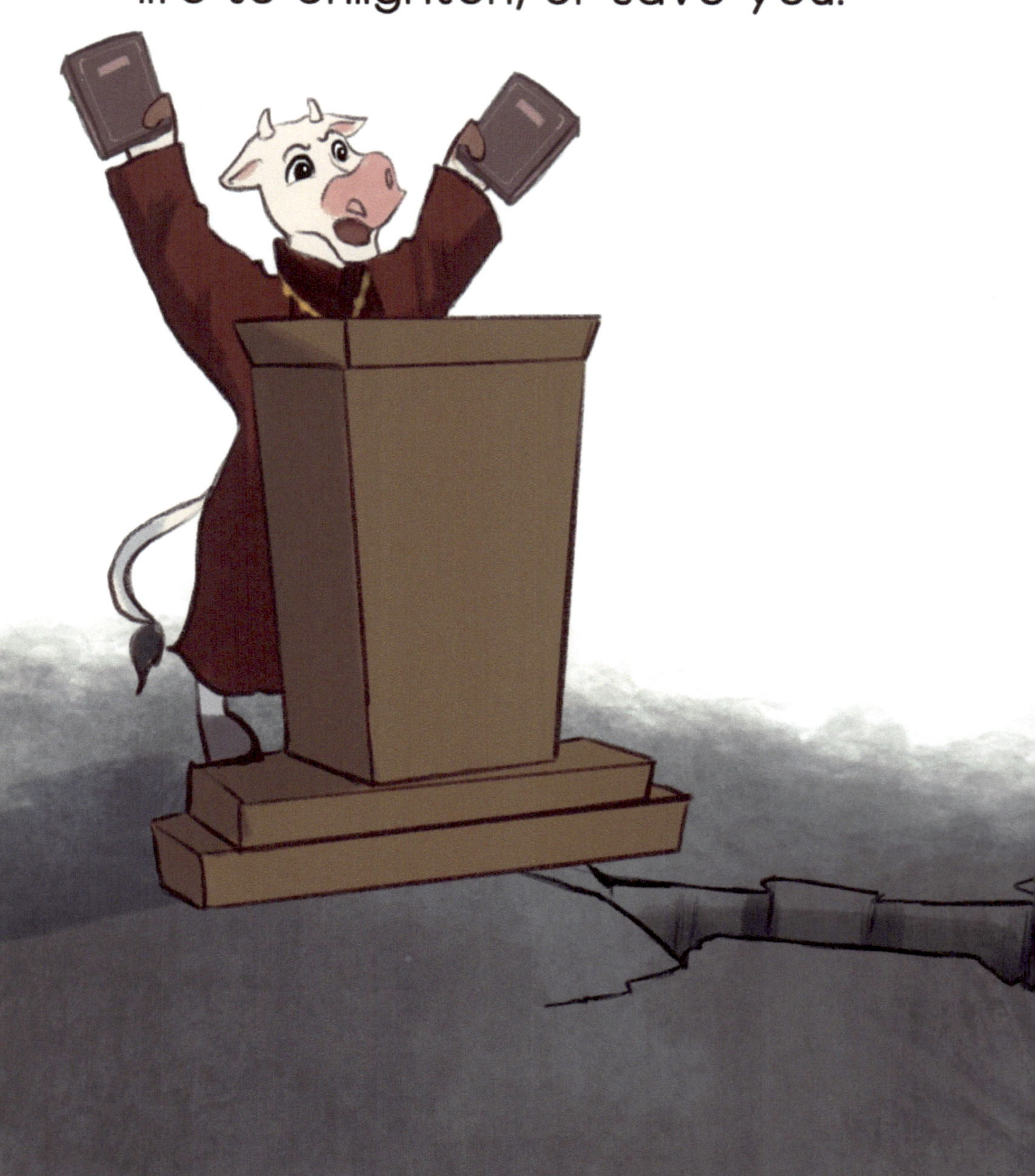

They're peddled by mostly unholy middlemen who divide, steal, disempower, and screw.

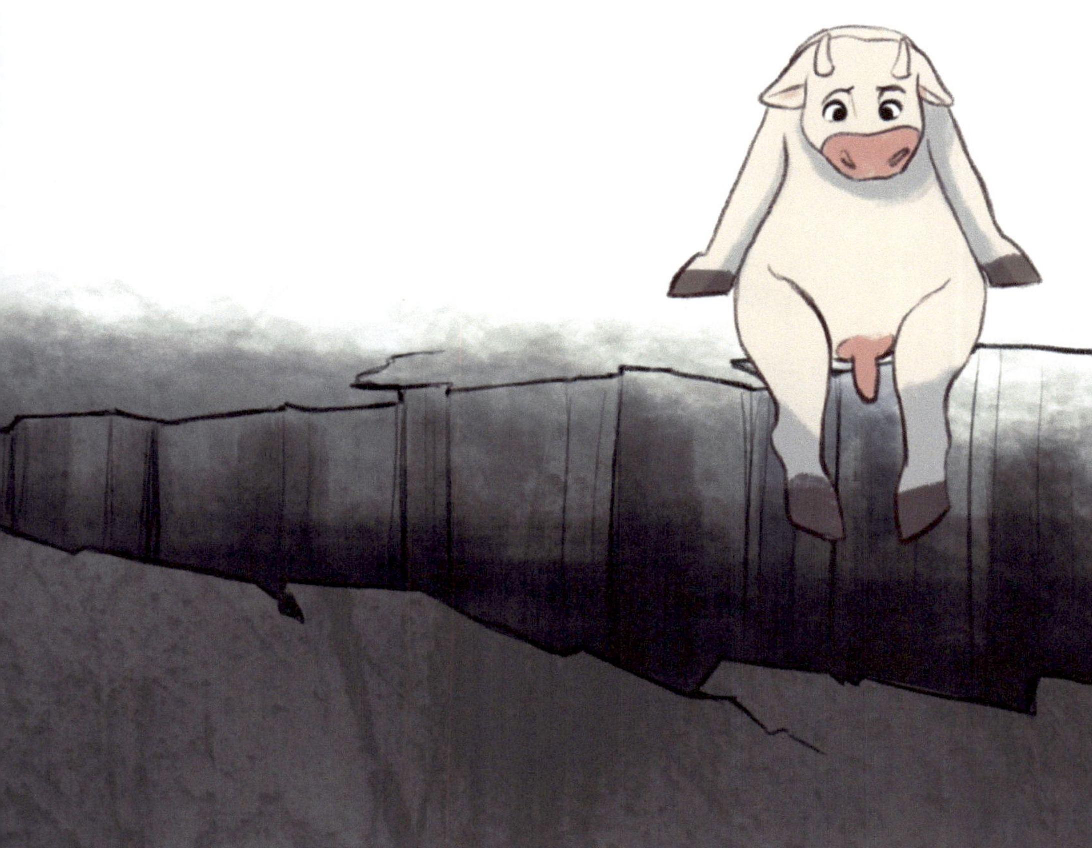

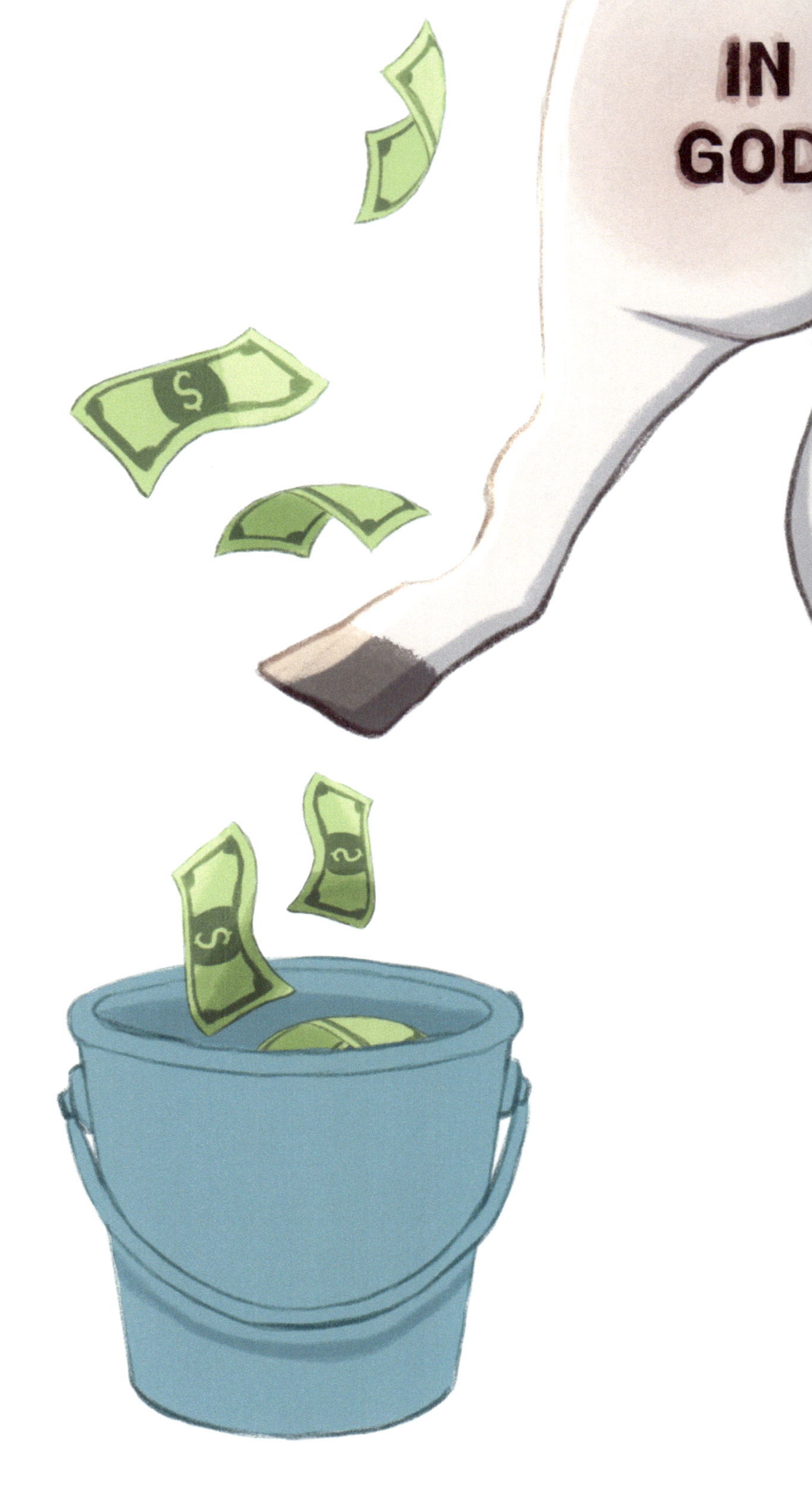
IN
GOD

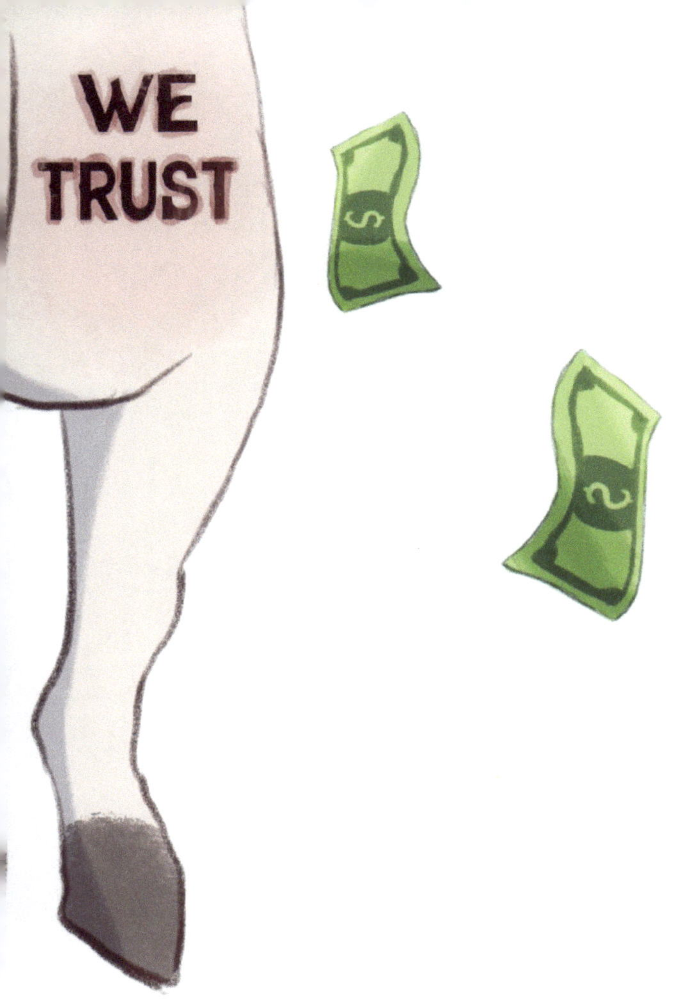

Never trust those who are self-branded 'In God We Trust', and question their authority and hypocrisy, always.

You weren't born brain-dead, so for Christ-sakes, wake the fuck up from your comatose malaise.

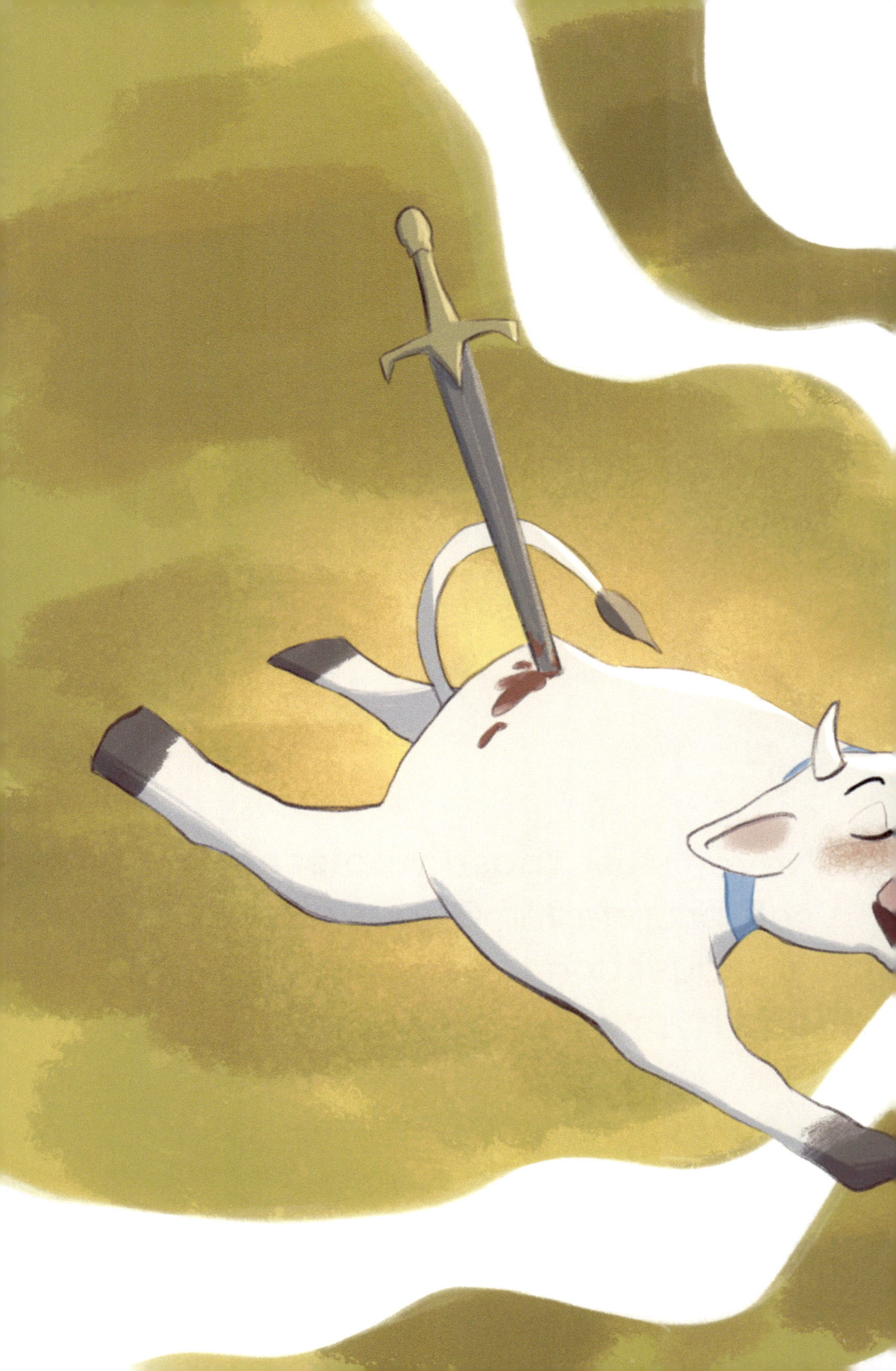

You ought to be grateful for each day you're alive, being self-anointed as sacred.

So, don't take yourself for granted as many admirers find you delicious being naked.

Your fertility and life-giving qualities are your blessing not to waste away until you die.

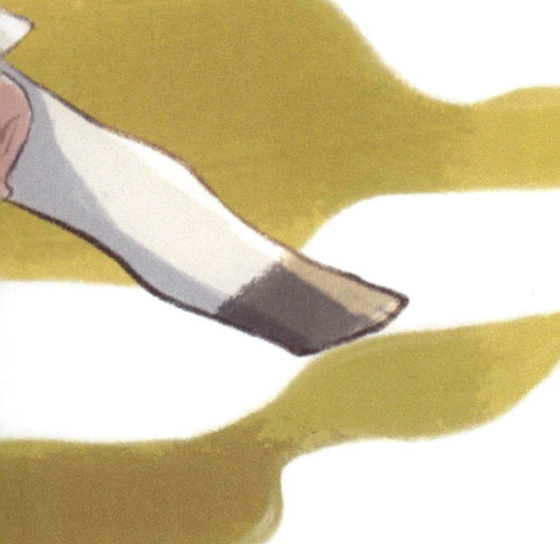

Maybe if you wake the fuck up, you'll spend each day being your true self and not live a lie.

The mystical soothsayers on your farm know the value of balance to survive.

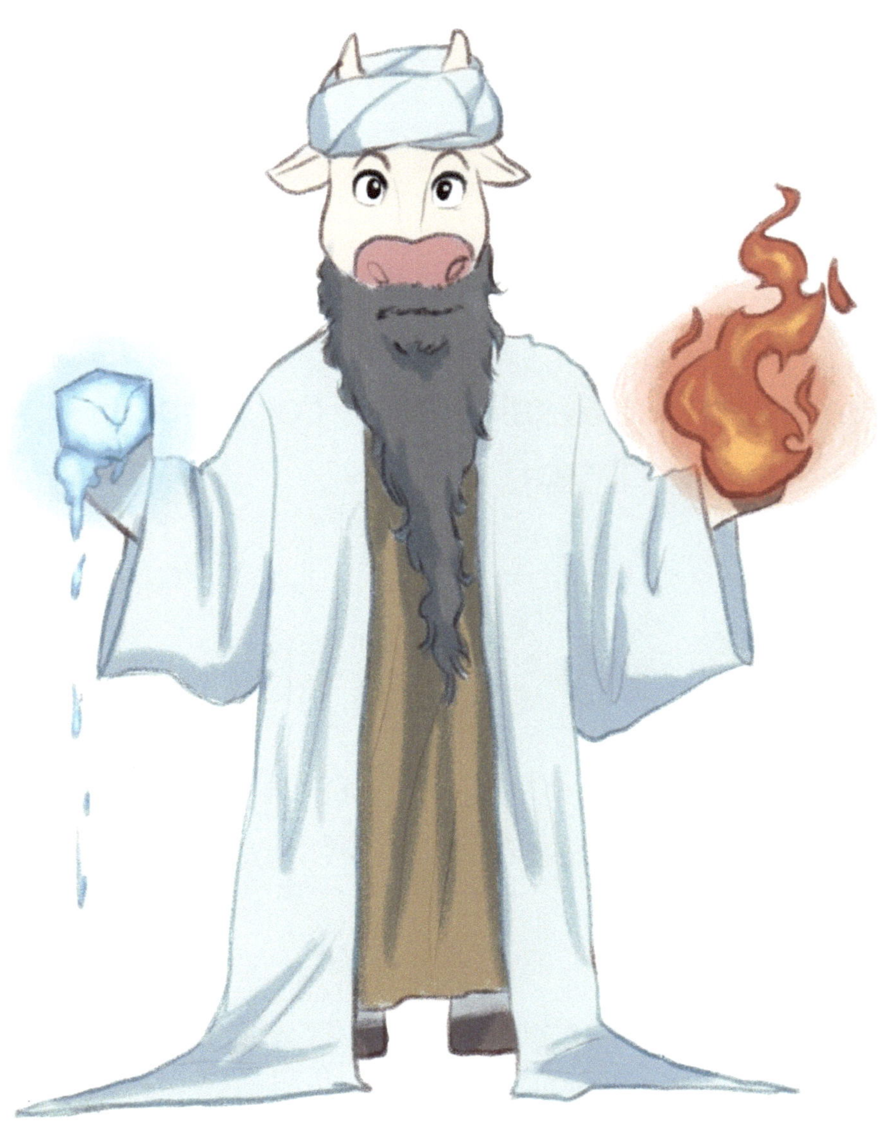

Science even proves how the cosmos rely on the laws of equilibrium to thrive.

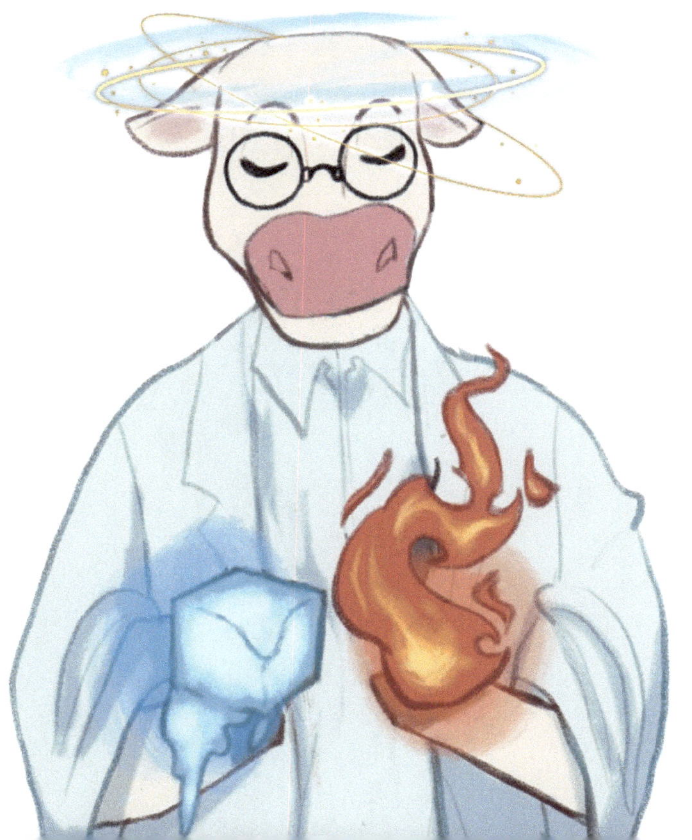

Now say, what's the deal with being hyper-stimulated and attached to those radioactive toys everywhere you go?

How about you fucking wake up, get smarter and not turn into a dumb-ass so unsocial and faux.

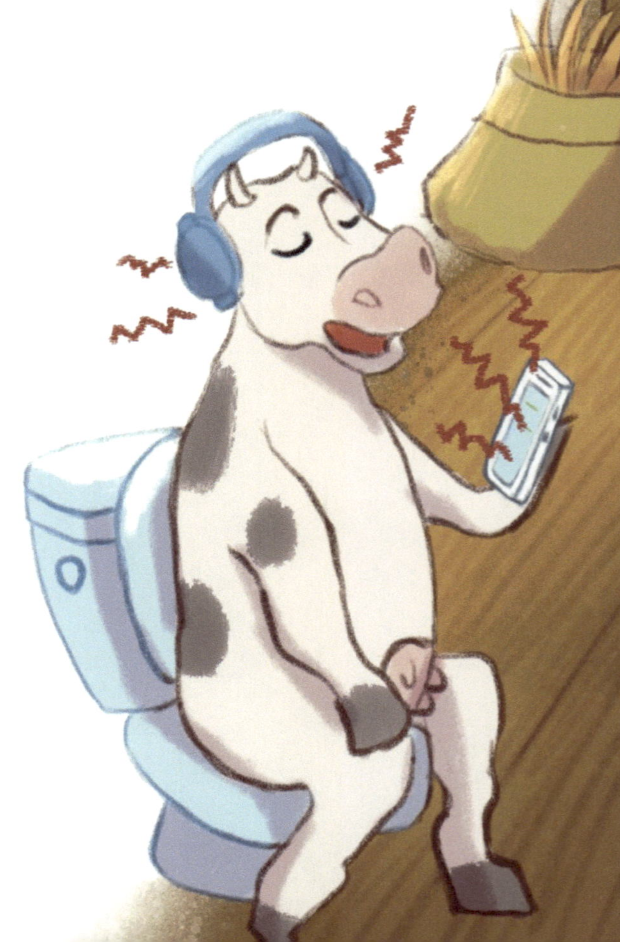

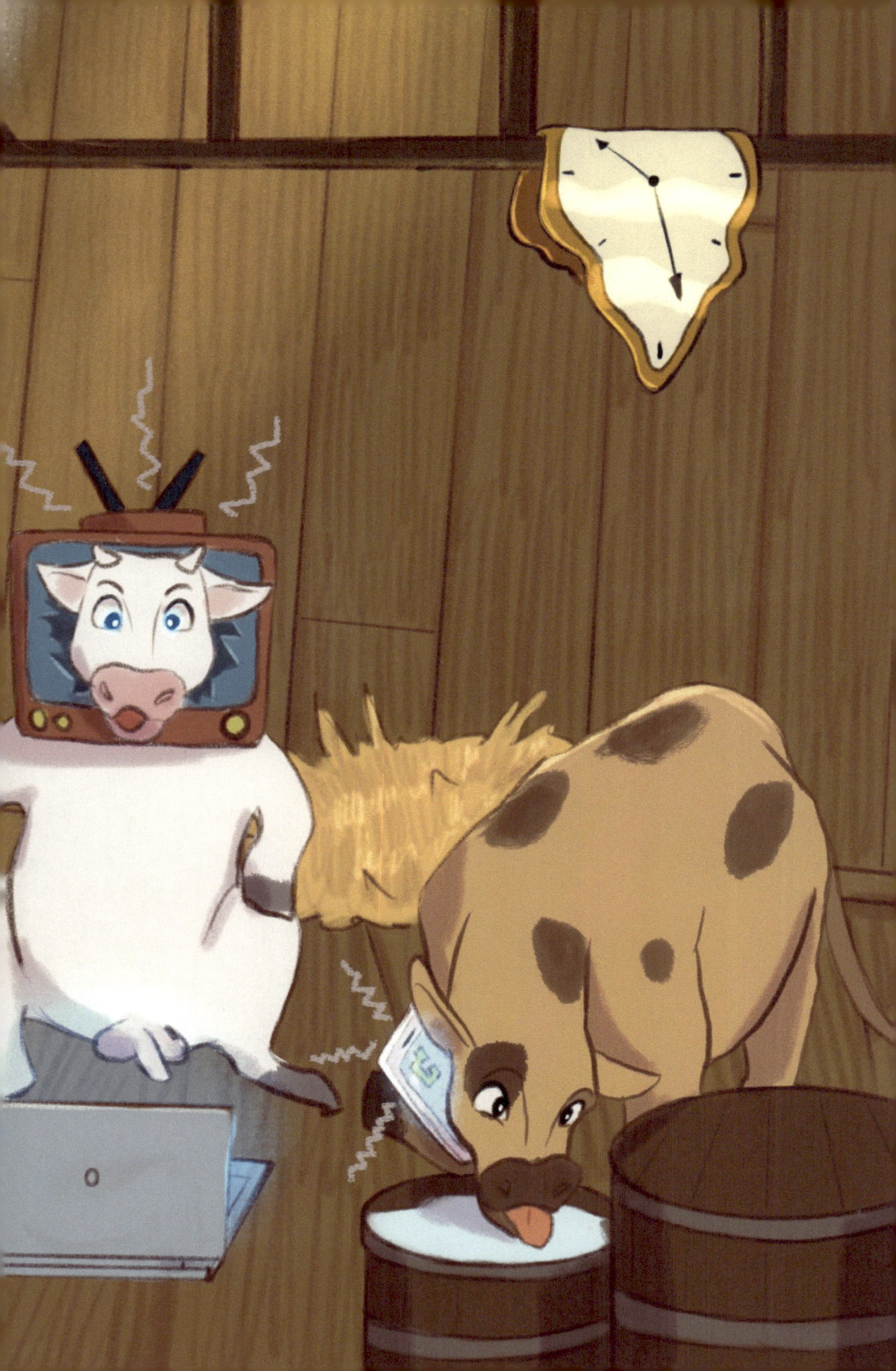

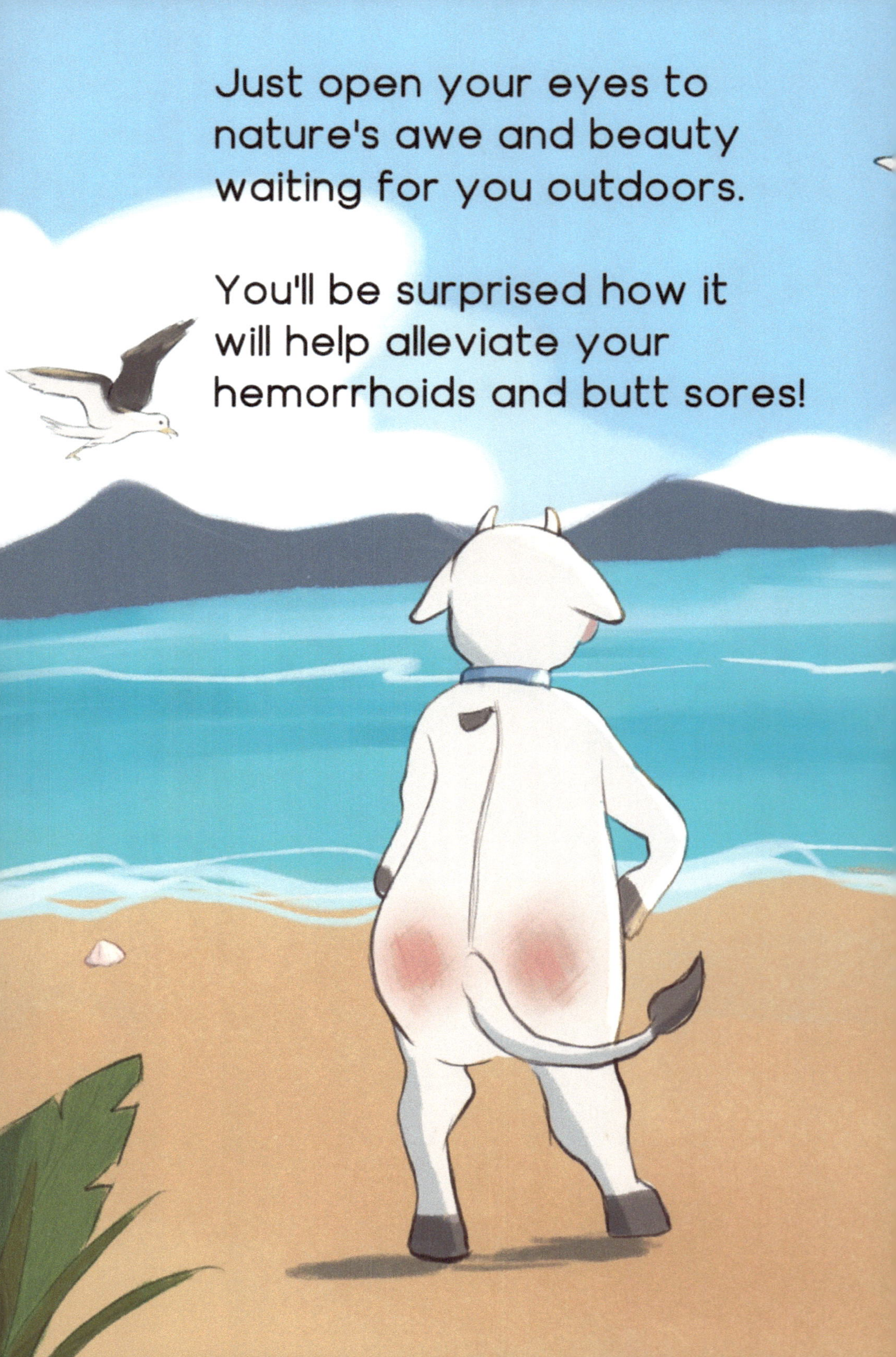

Just open your eyes to nature's awe and beauty waiting for you outdoors.

You'll be surprised how it will help alleviate your hemorrhoids and butt sores!

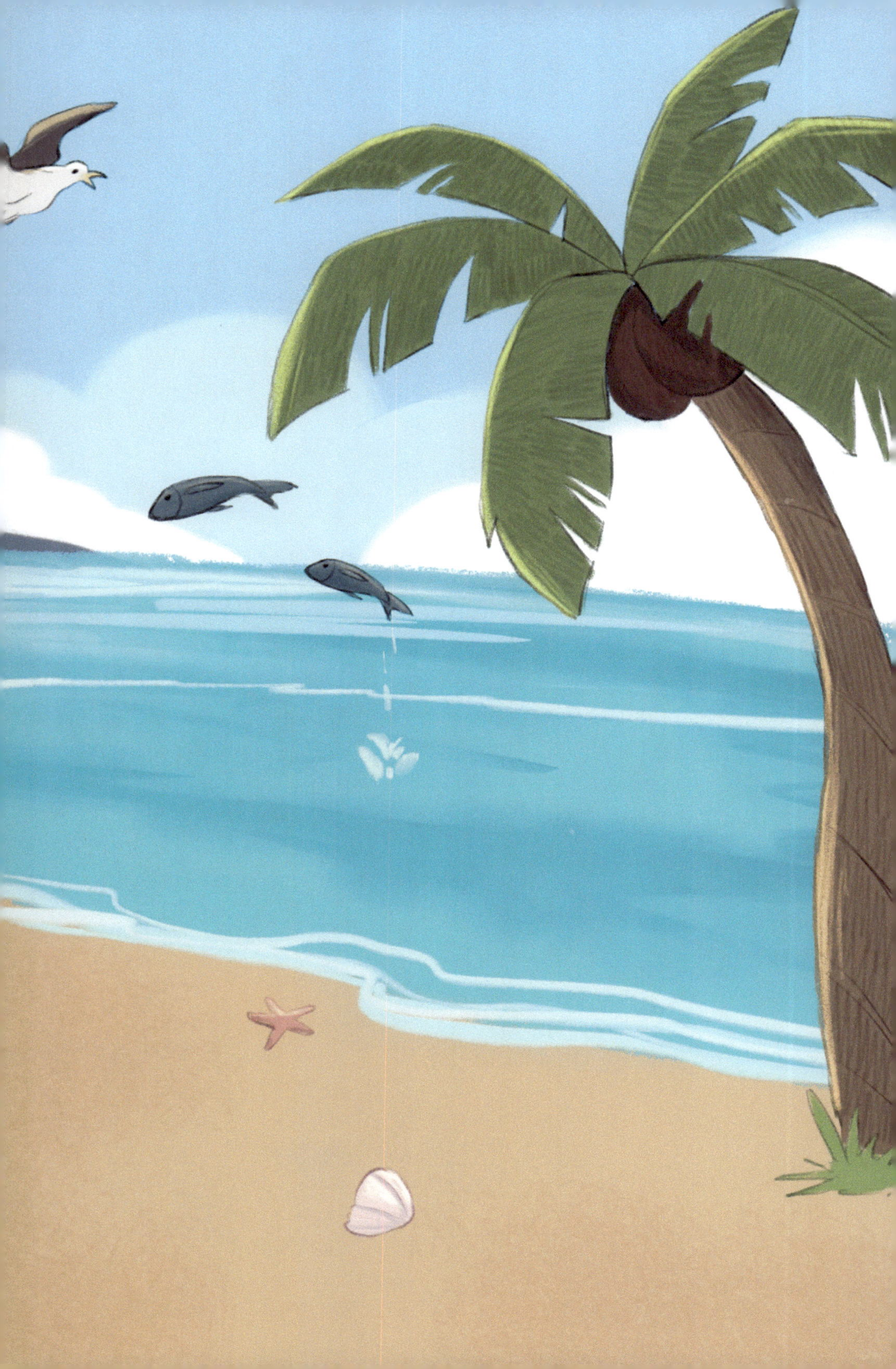

You know that all your distractions and lazy comforts come with a heavy price.

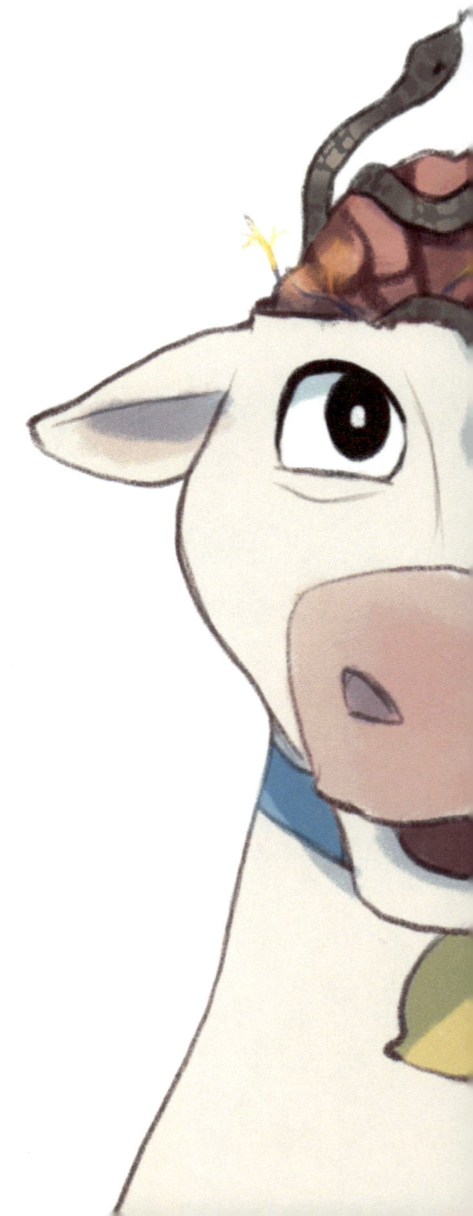

You're just inducing harm to yourself by feeding the bad juju into your highly complex spongy device.

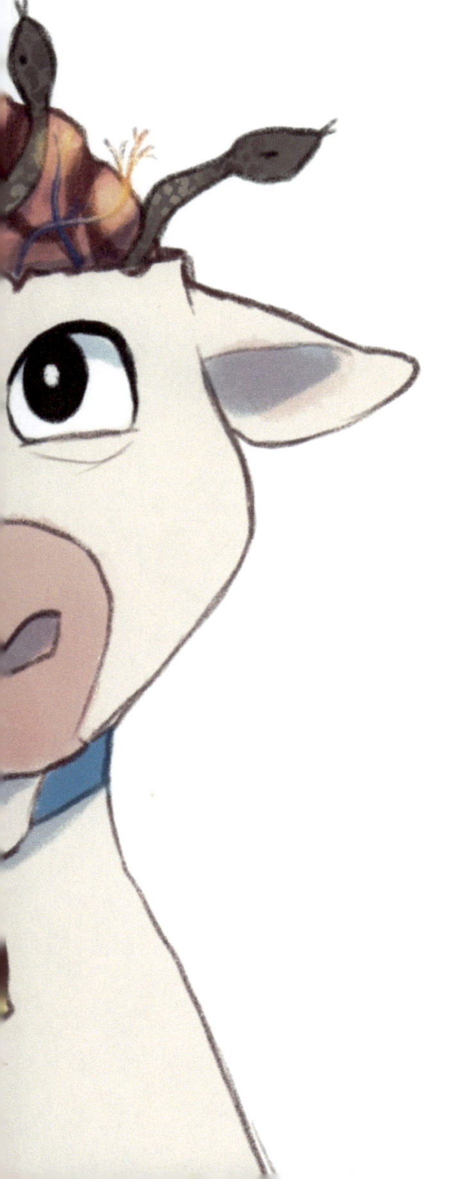

When you were in your mama, you had no anxiety, depression or PTSD you know.

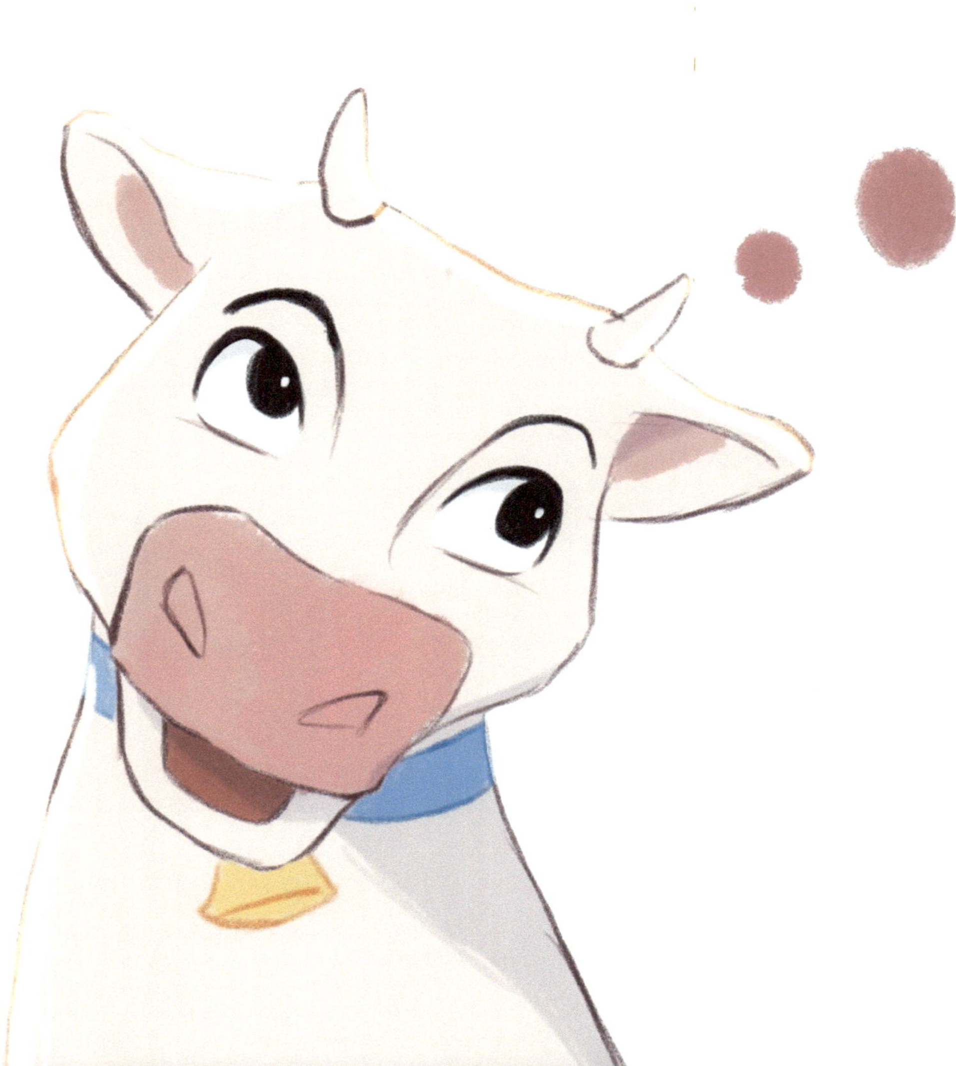

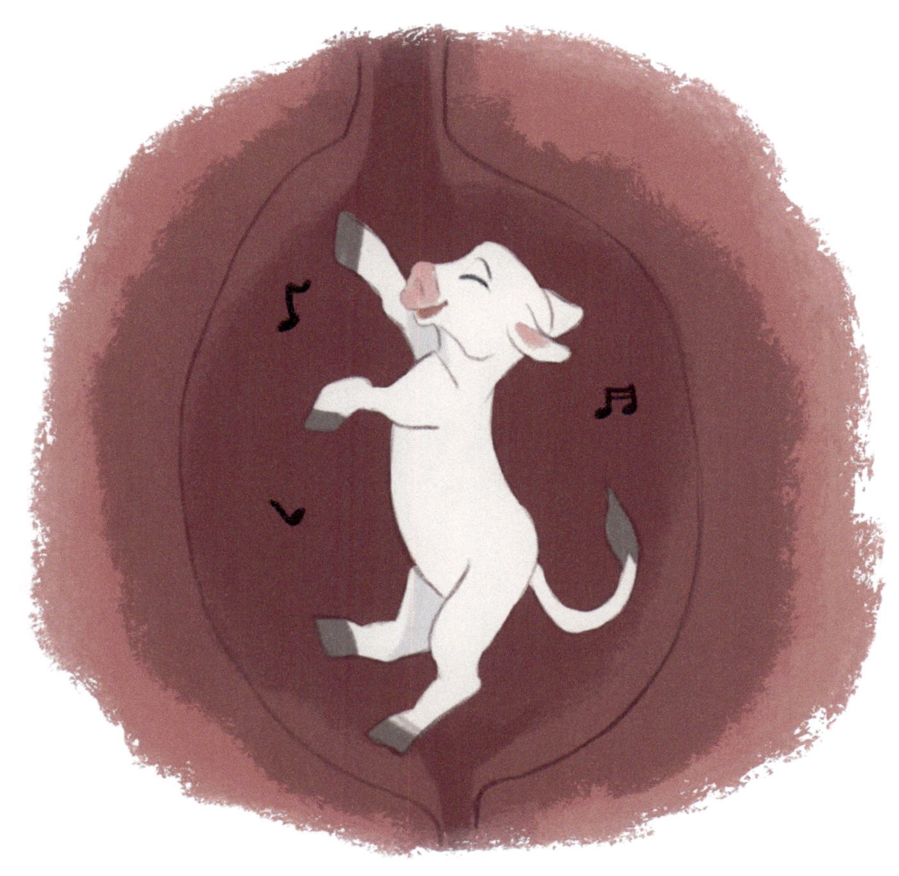

You danced, played, and sang incessantly, so wake up you fuck and be that badass aglow.

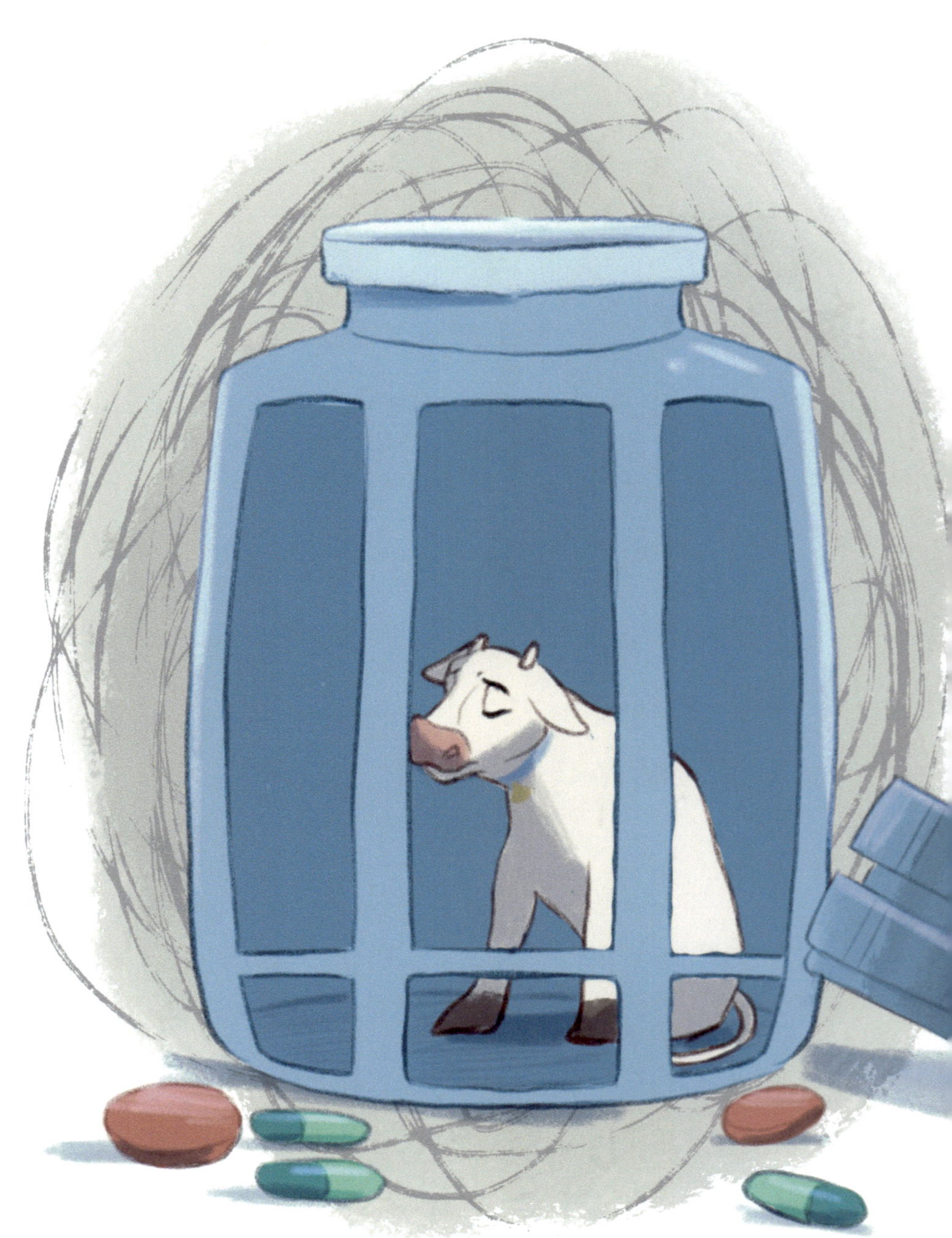

There's more to living than being a sadfuck, who's self-medicated and isolated.

Life goes fast, so you best moove your ass and get yourself quickly liberated.

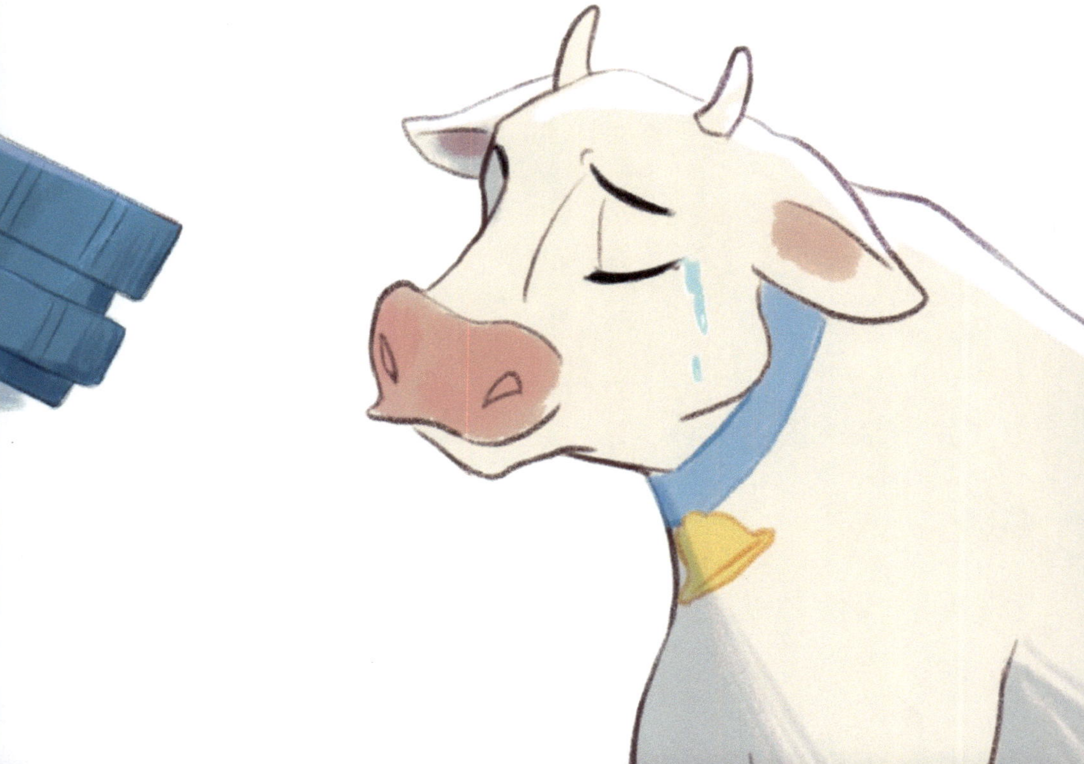

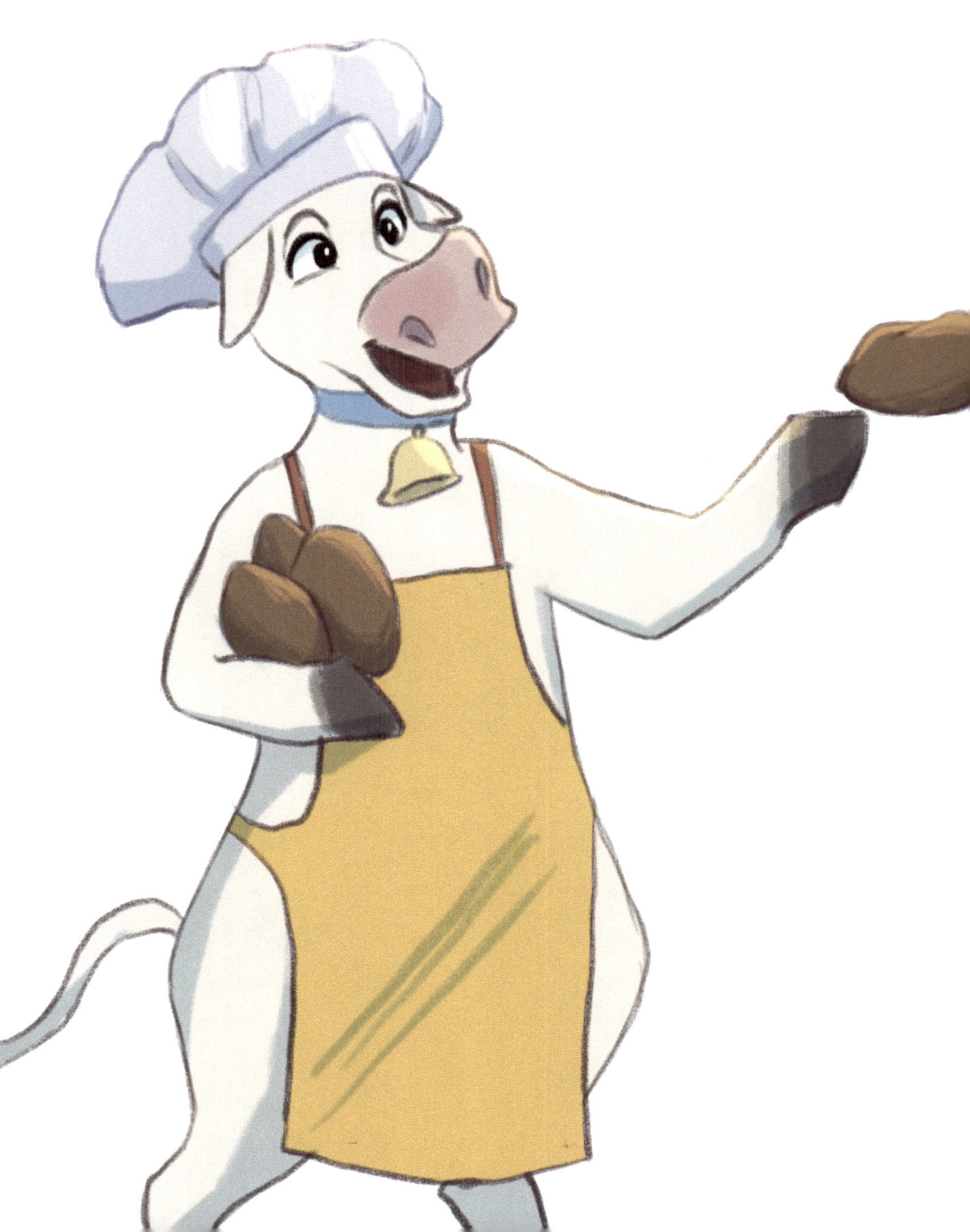

You can't take yourself too seriously, so laugh it all off and enjoy your short trip here.

Maybe if you wake the fuck up from within, you wouldn't be so fucked by Mr. Fear.

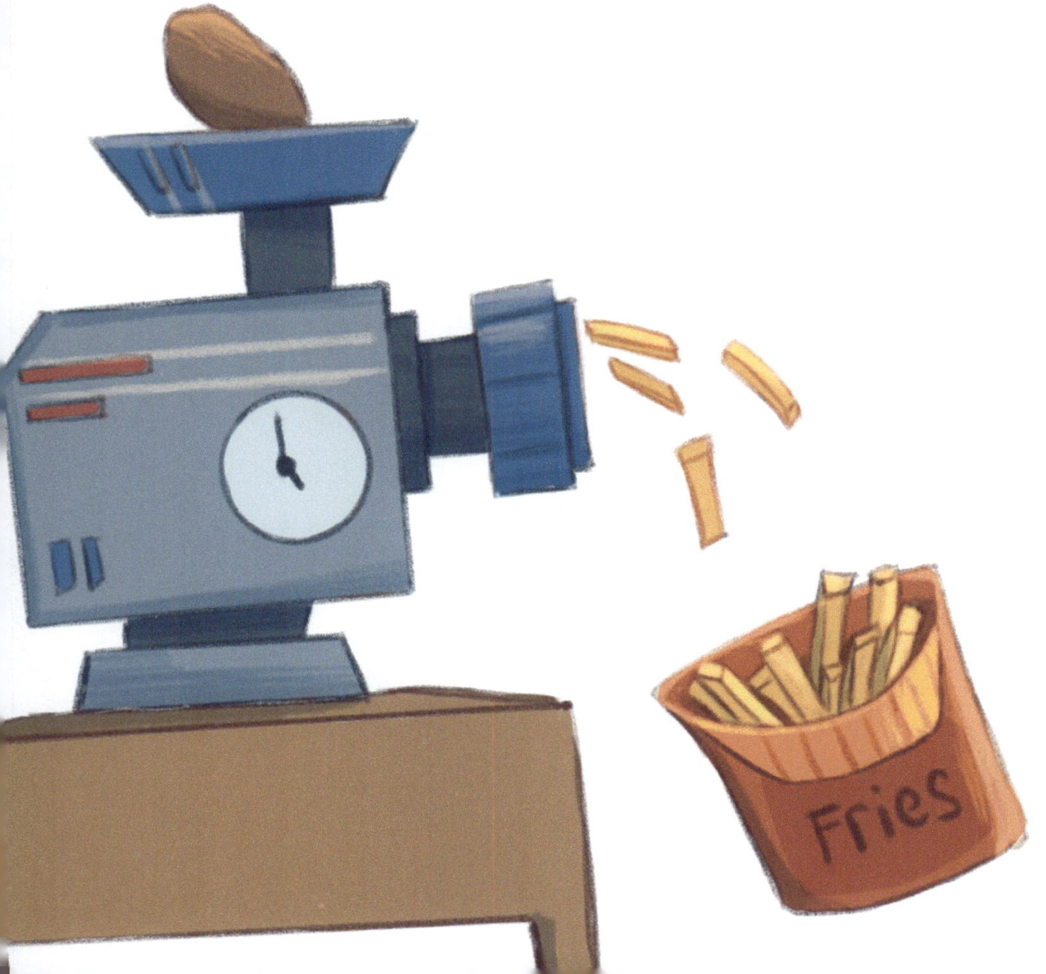

What are you afraid of anyway, the way to happiness is not being chained to anything or anyone.

it's about having passion in what you do, looking forward to something, and loving someone.

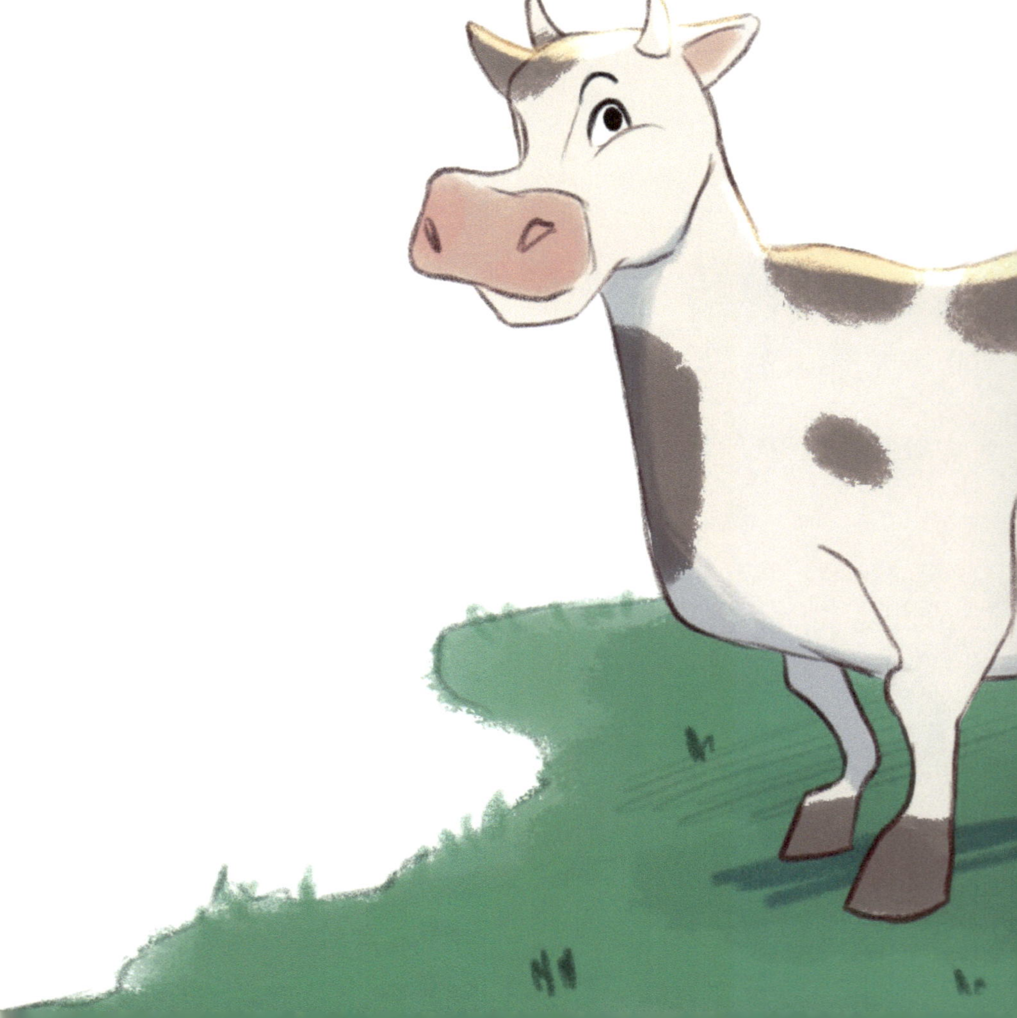

You already had great practice with all of that for nine months before you busted your way out.

Don't you want to wake the fuck up now, and wipe that brown slimy crap off your snout?

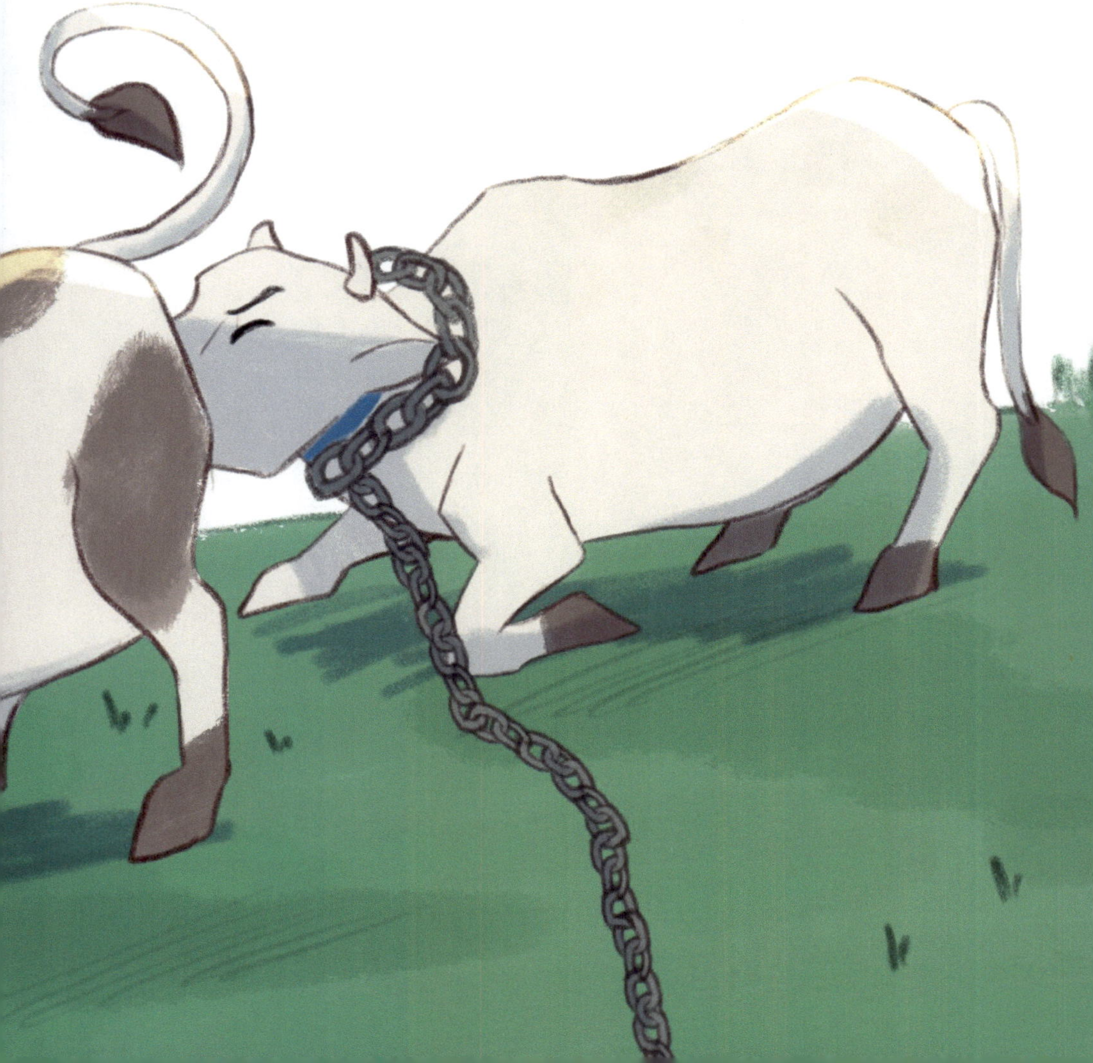

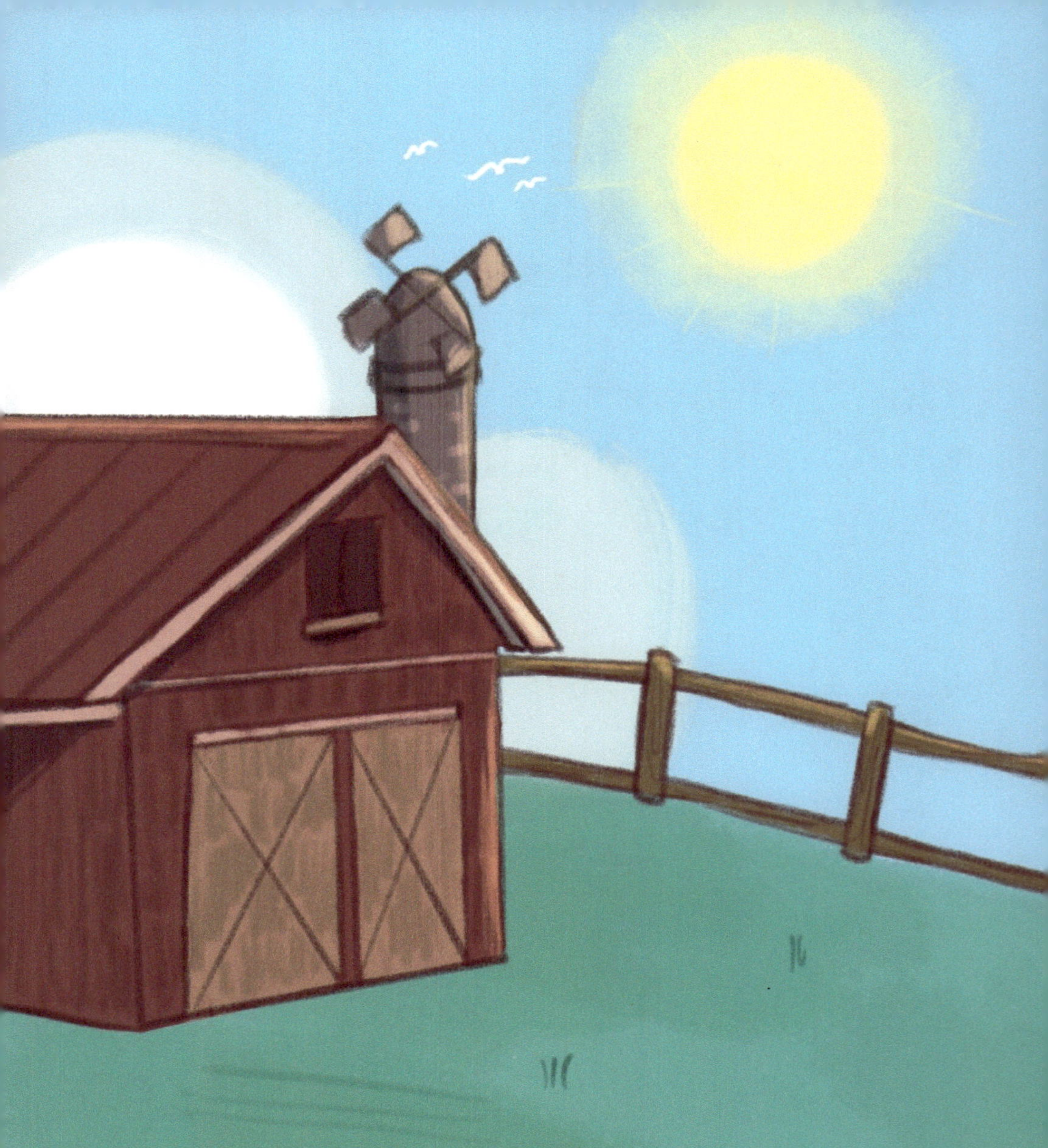

Hey beautiful one, you were so much more aware, alive, and in-Spirit being inside your mama's womb.

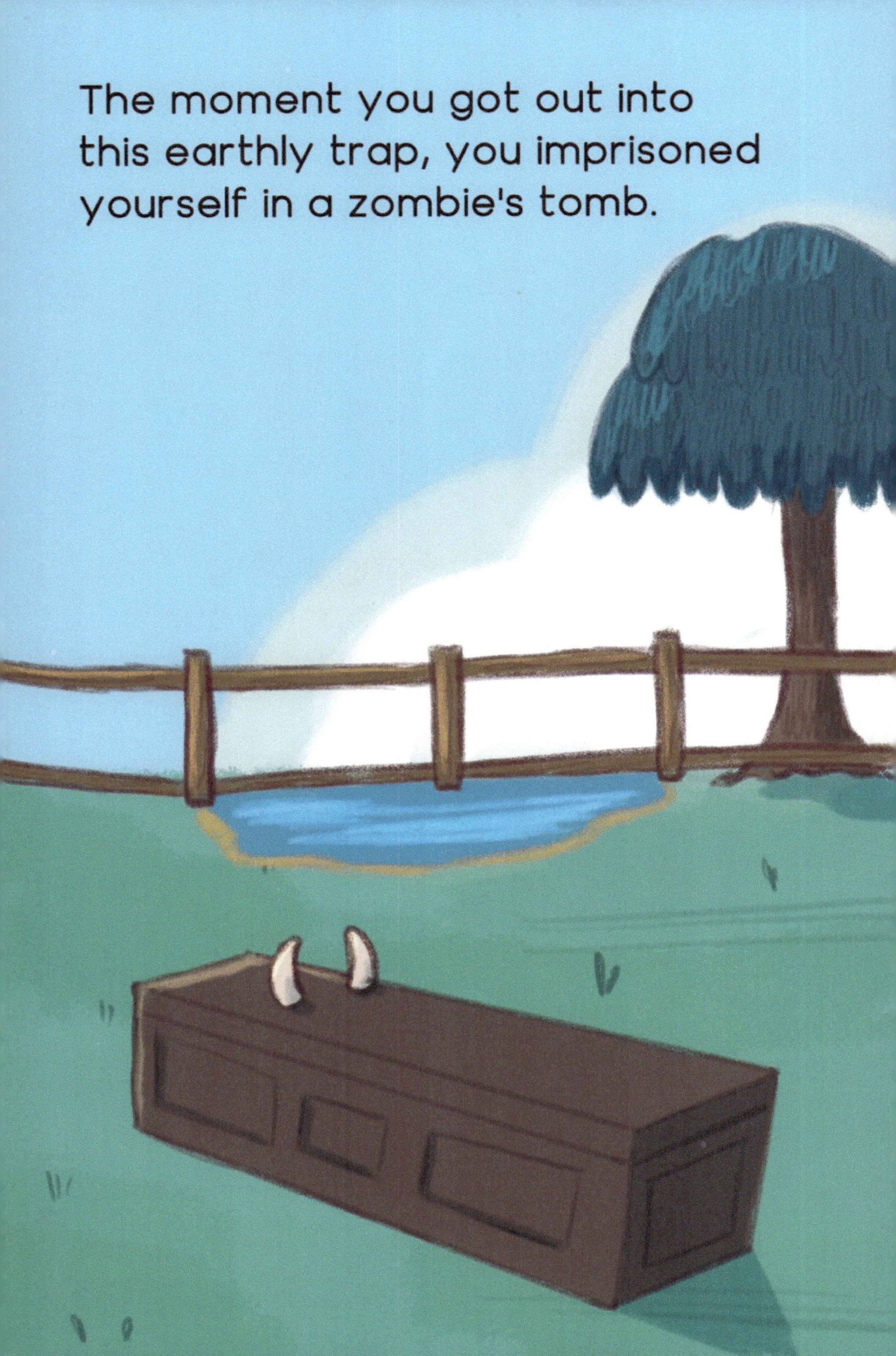
The moment you got out into this earthly trap, you imprisoned yourself in a zombie's tomb.

Instead of loving yourself, you cowered up and justified your suffering as a sickly grownup.

Now, stop normalizing being comfortable drowning in your own dung, and wake the fuck up.

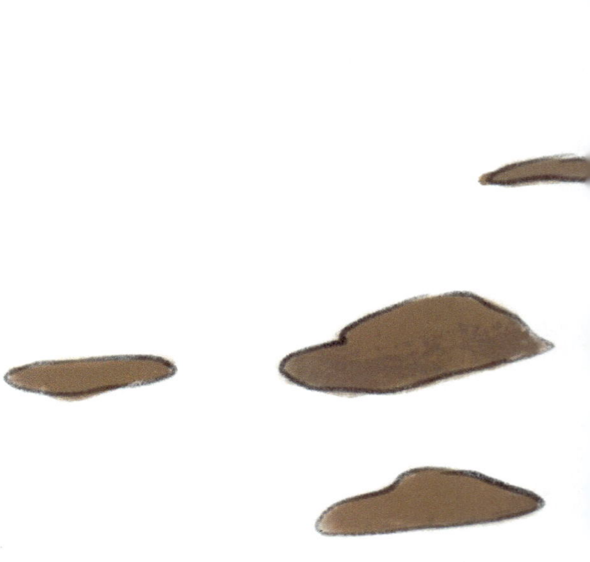

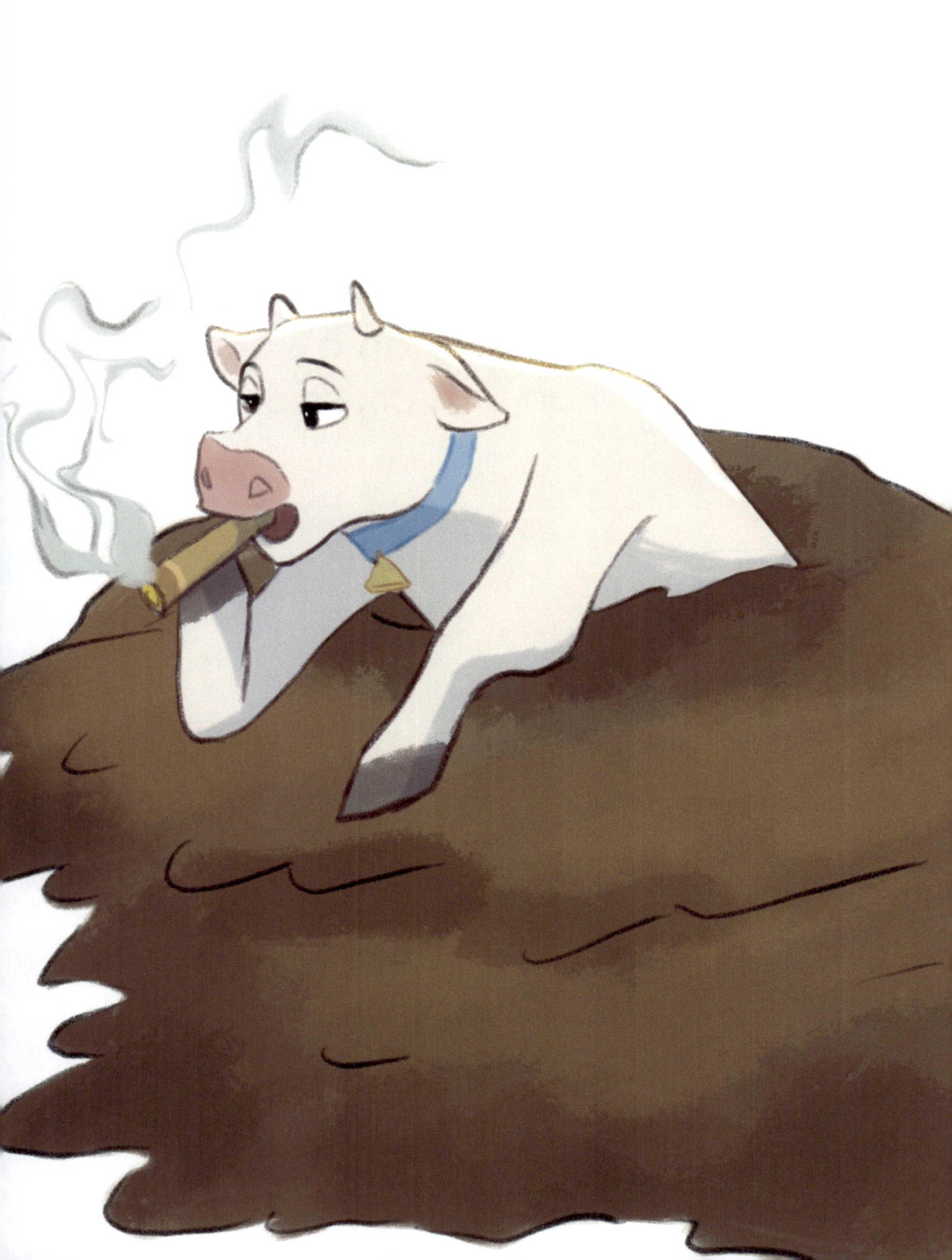

The good news is that you're still alive and are able to smell and feel the crap you made.

You can change yourself from a shitty state and be an awakened cow to lead an Om crusade.

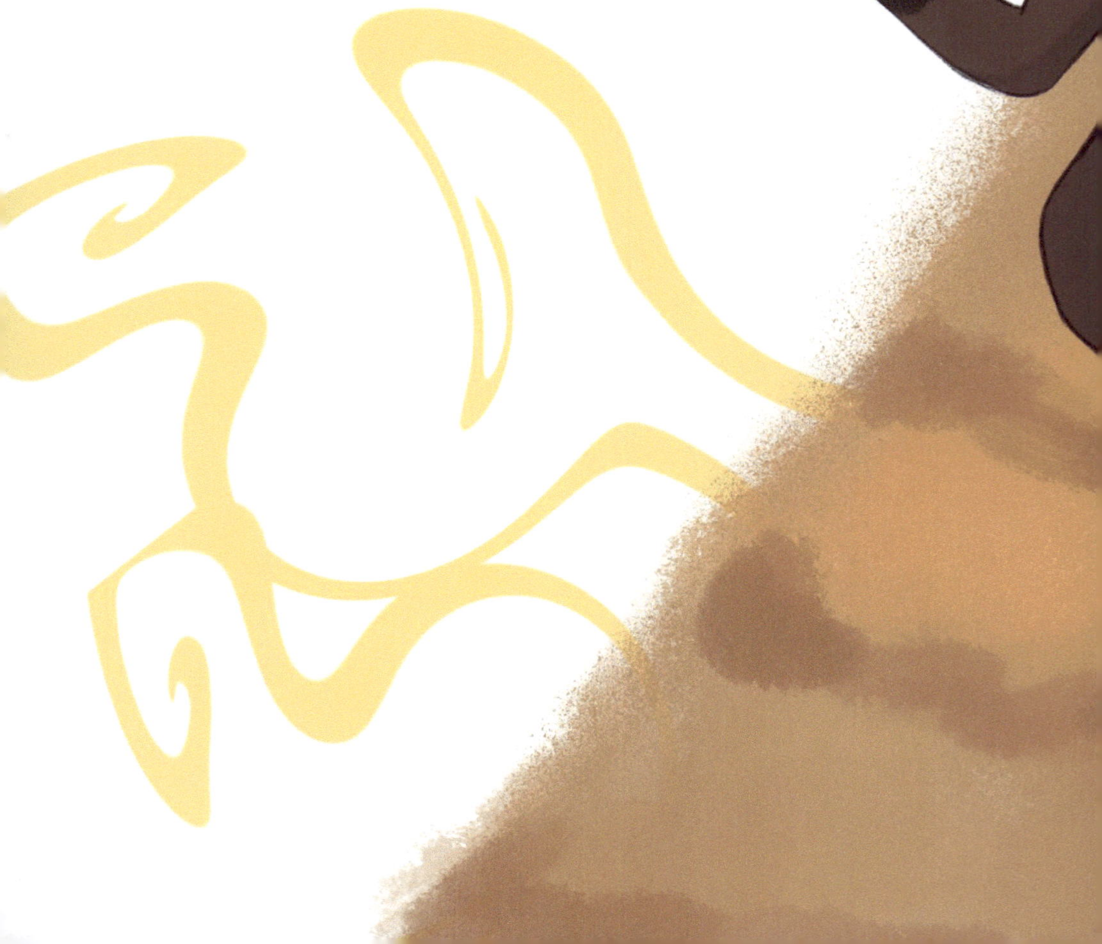

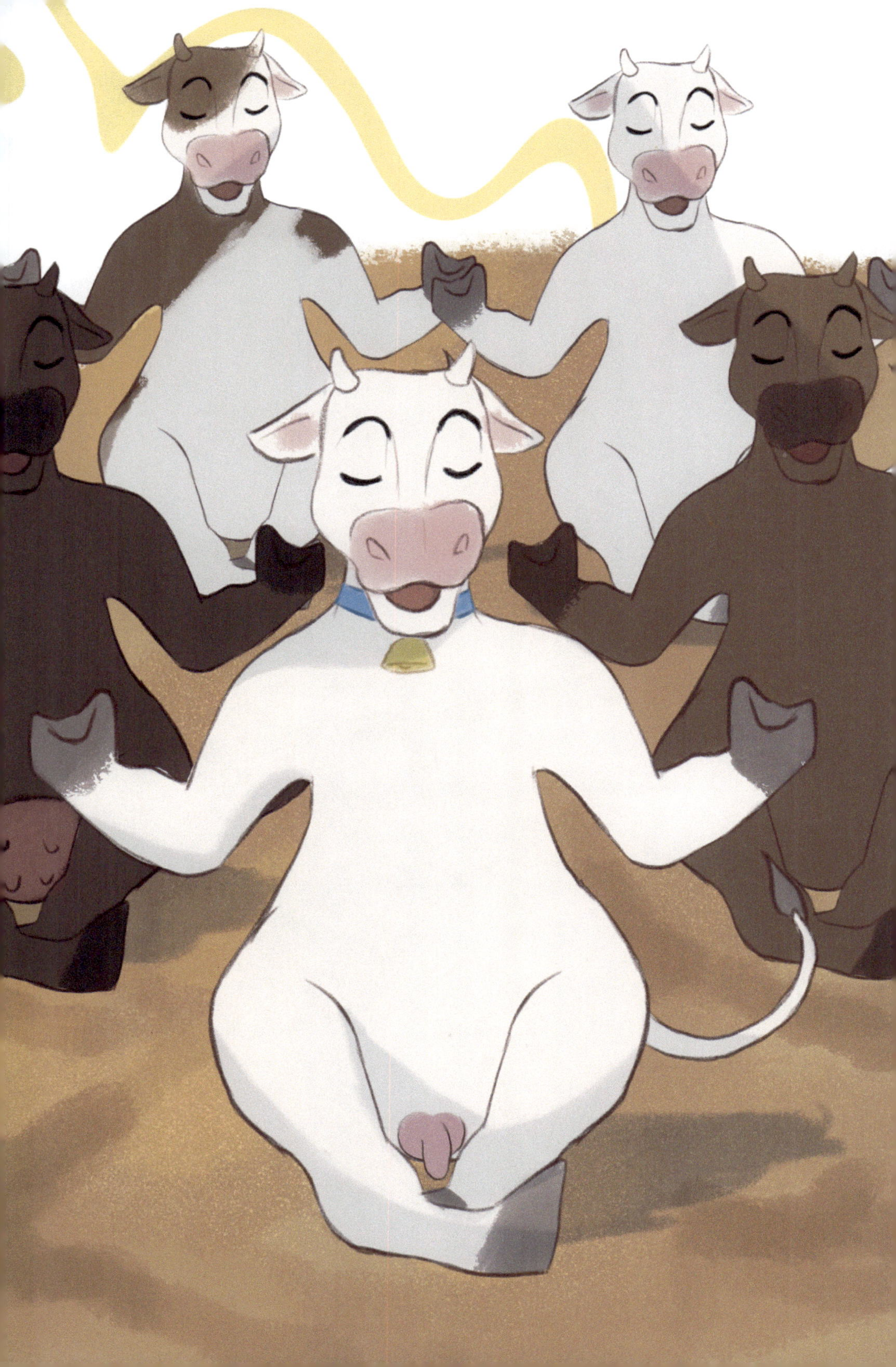

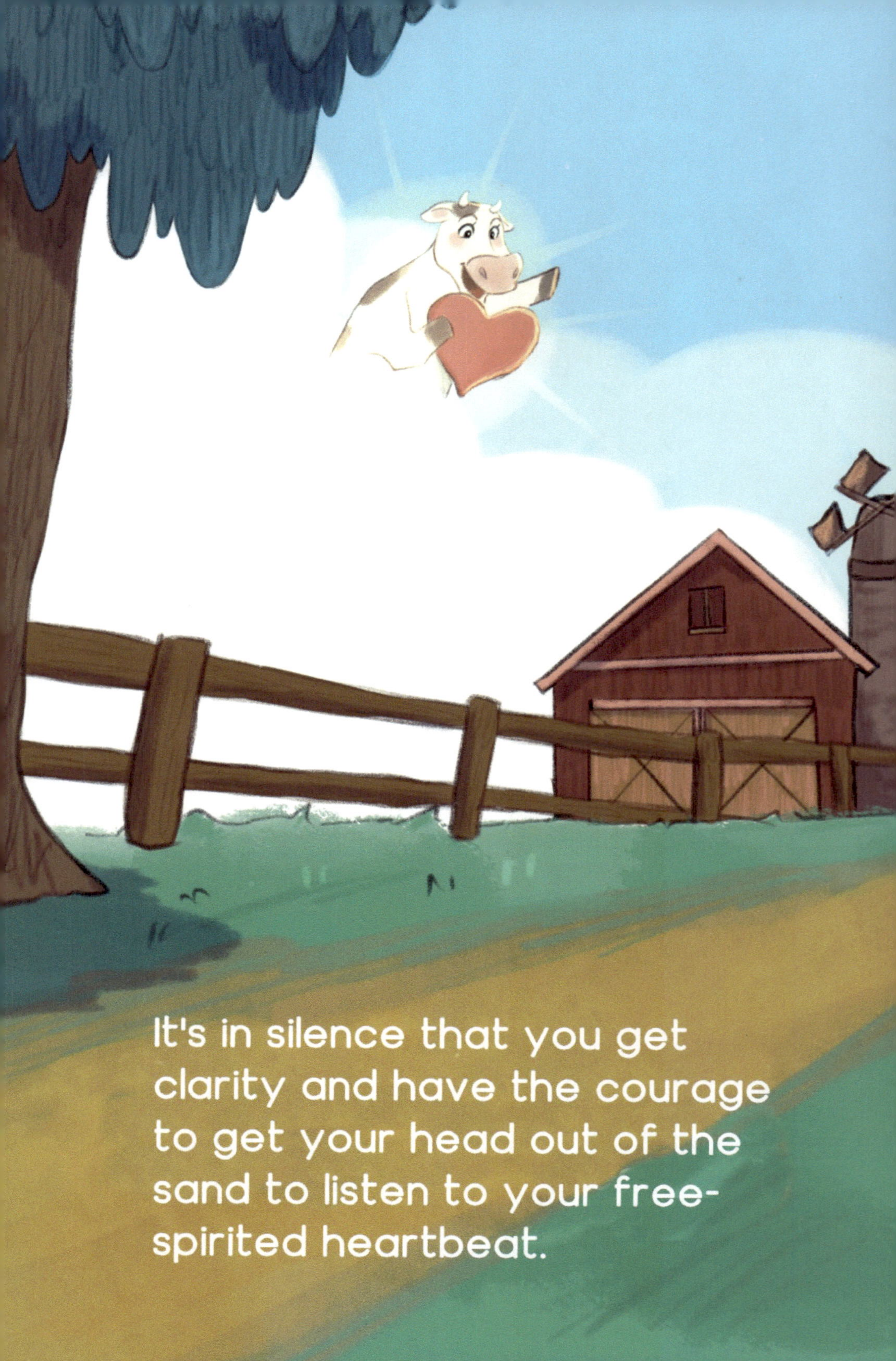

It's in silence that you get clarity and have the courage to get your head out of the sand to listen to your free-spirited heartbeat.

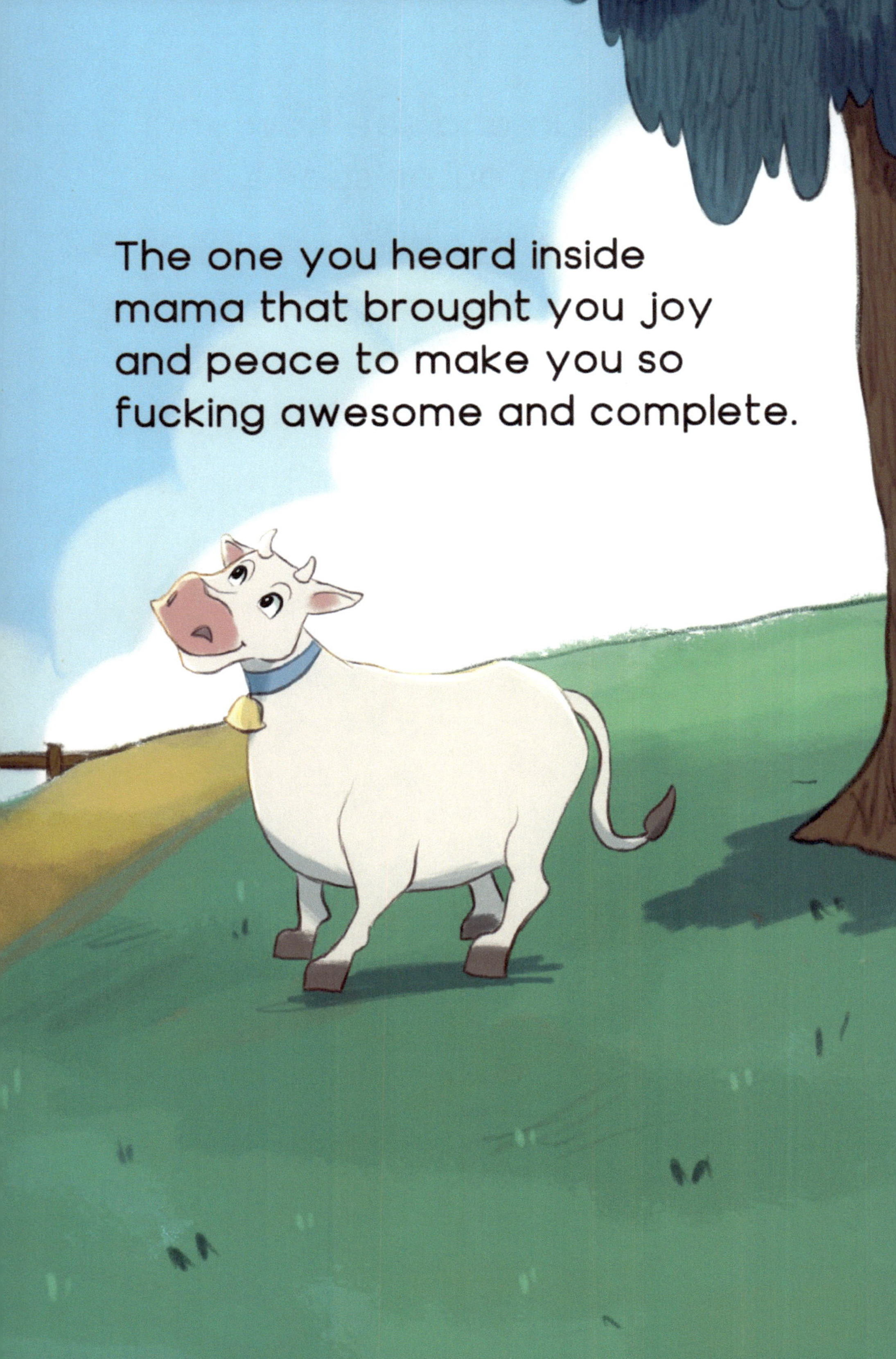

The one you heard inside mama that brought you joy and peace to make you so fucking awesome and complete.

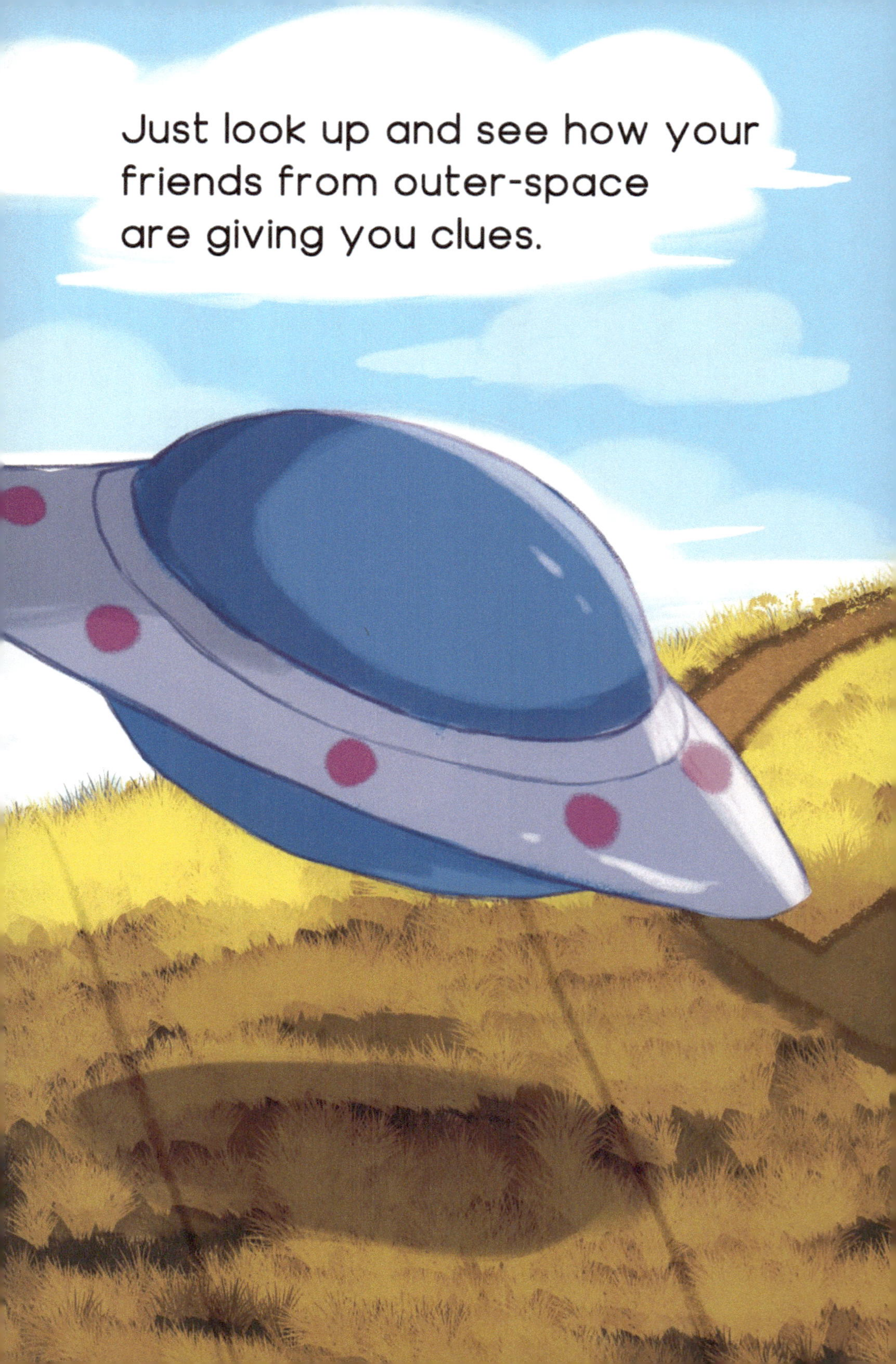

Just look up and see how your friends from outer-space are giving you clues.

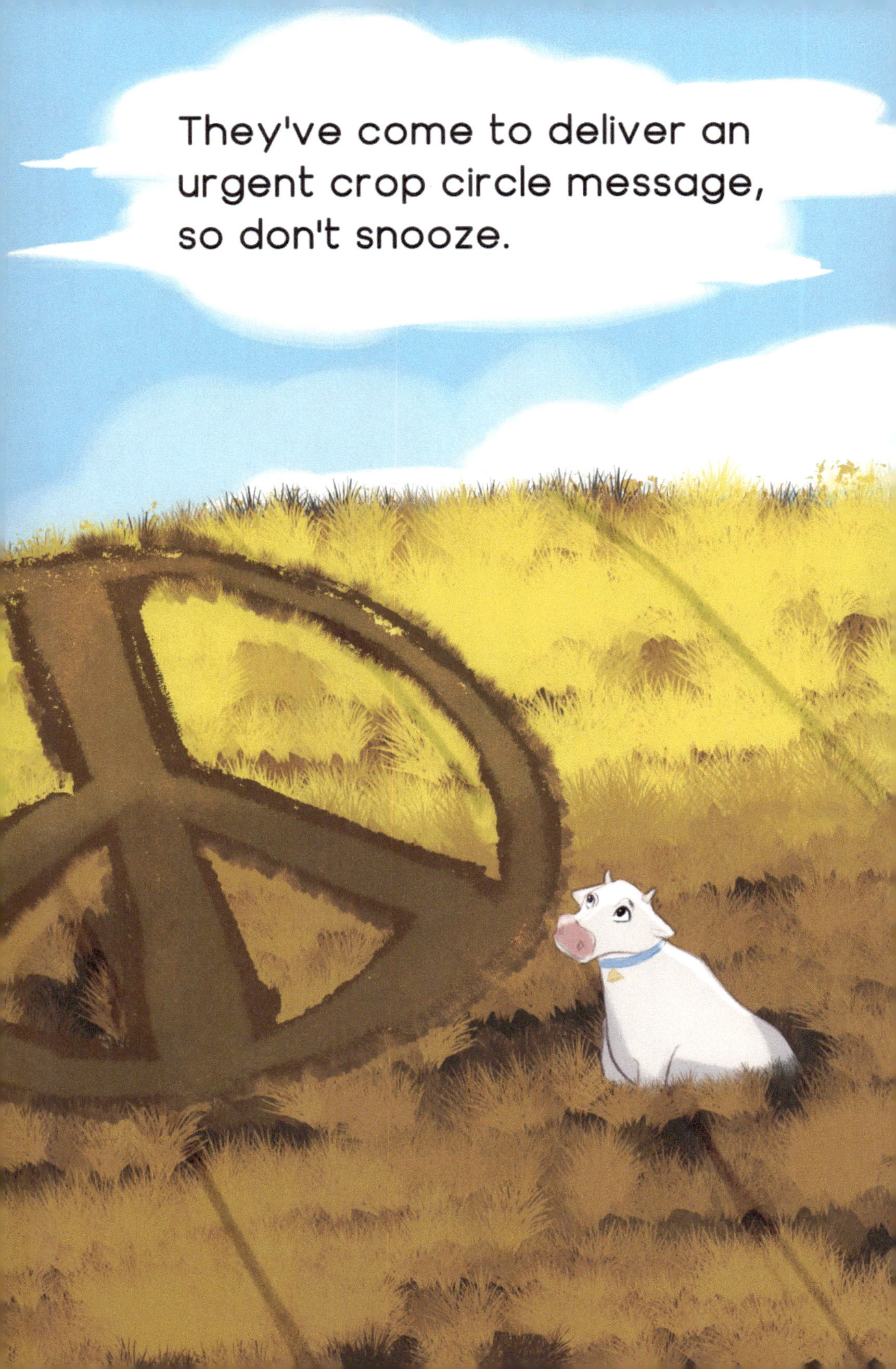

They've come to deliver an urgent crop circle message, so don't snooze.

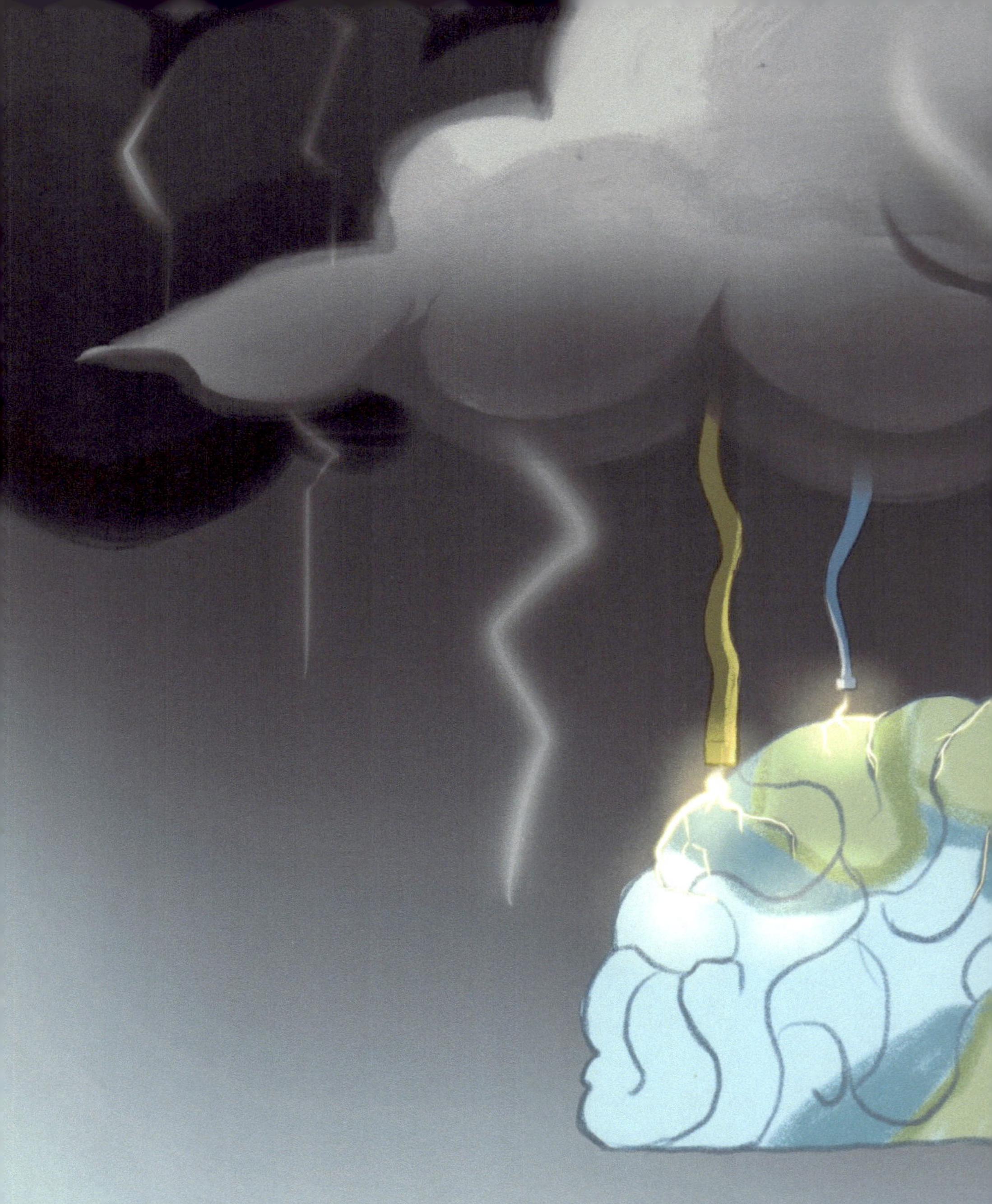

It's a sign from the universe that life on earth is in need of a major brain-bypass.

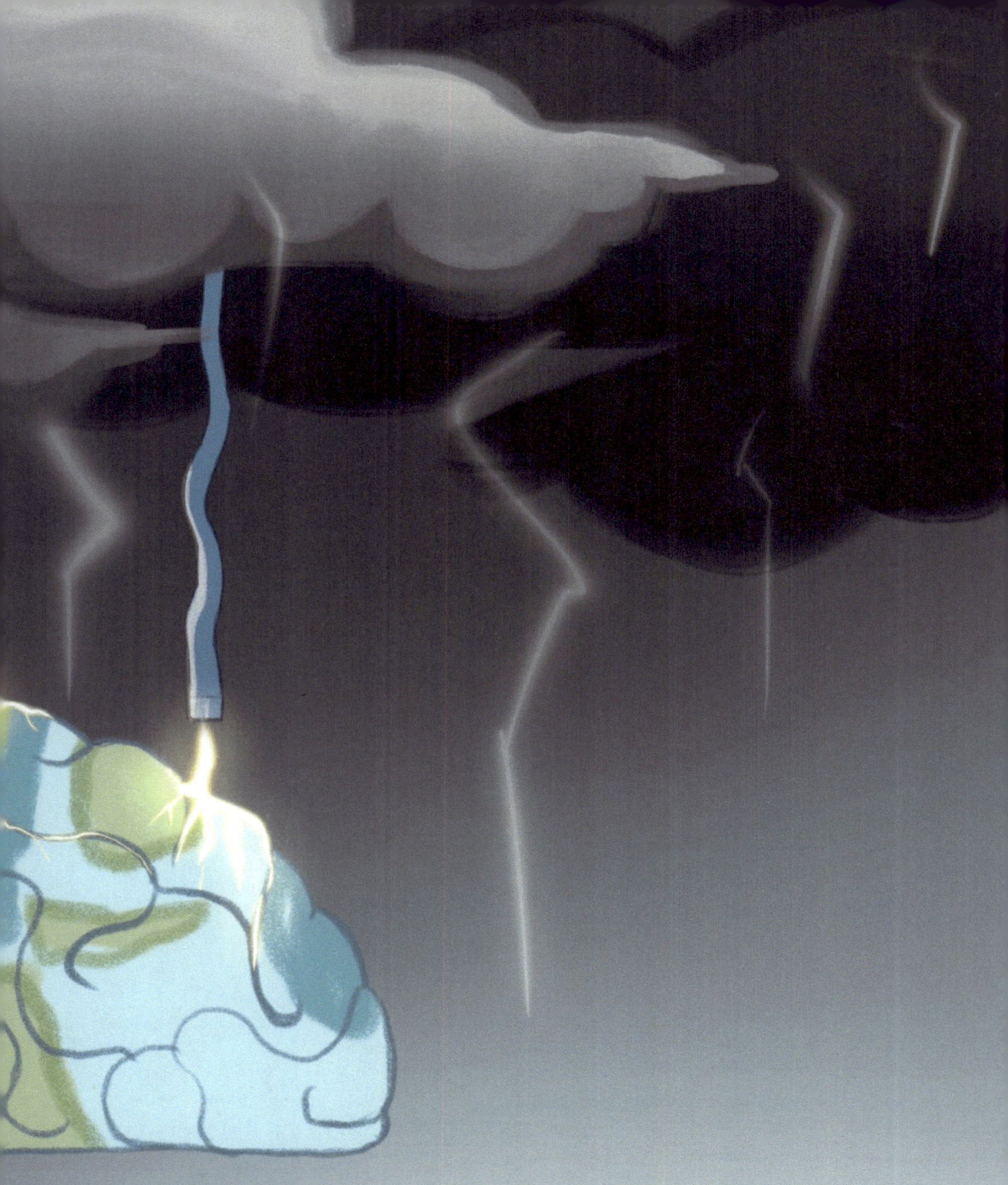

These beings want us all to wake the fuck up, before they zap our dumb-ass.

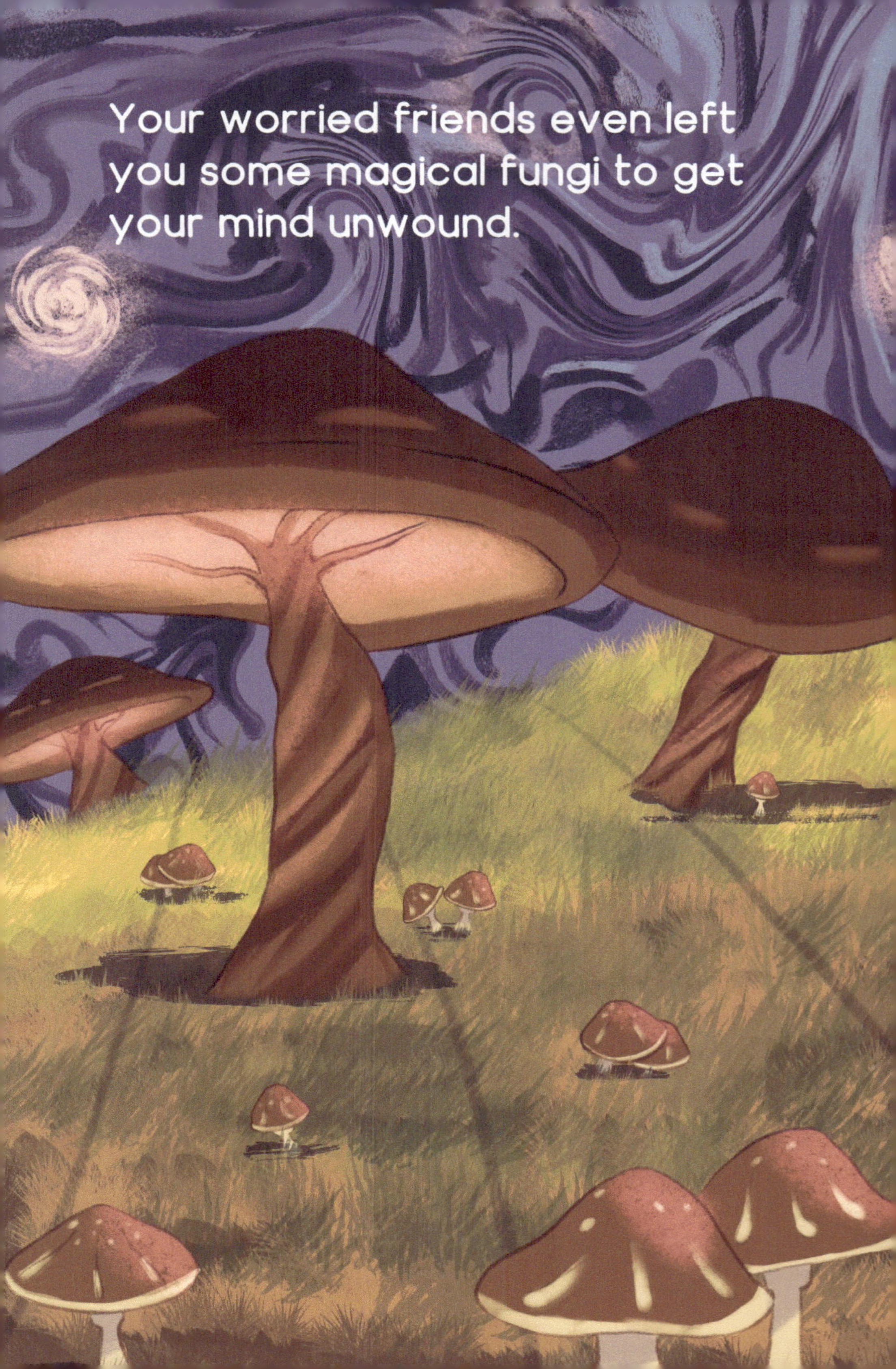

Your worried friends even left you some magical fungi to get your mind unwound.

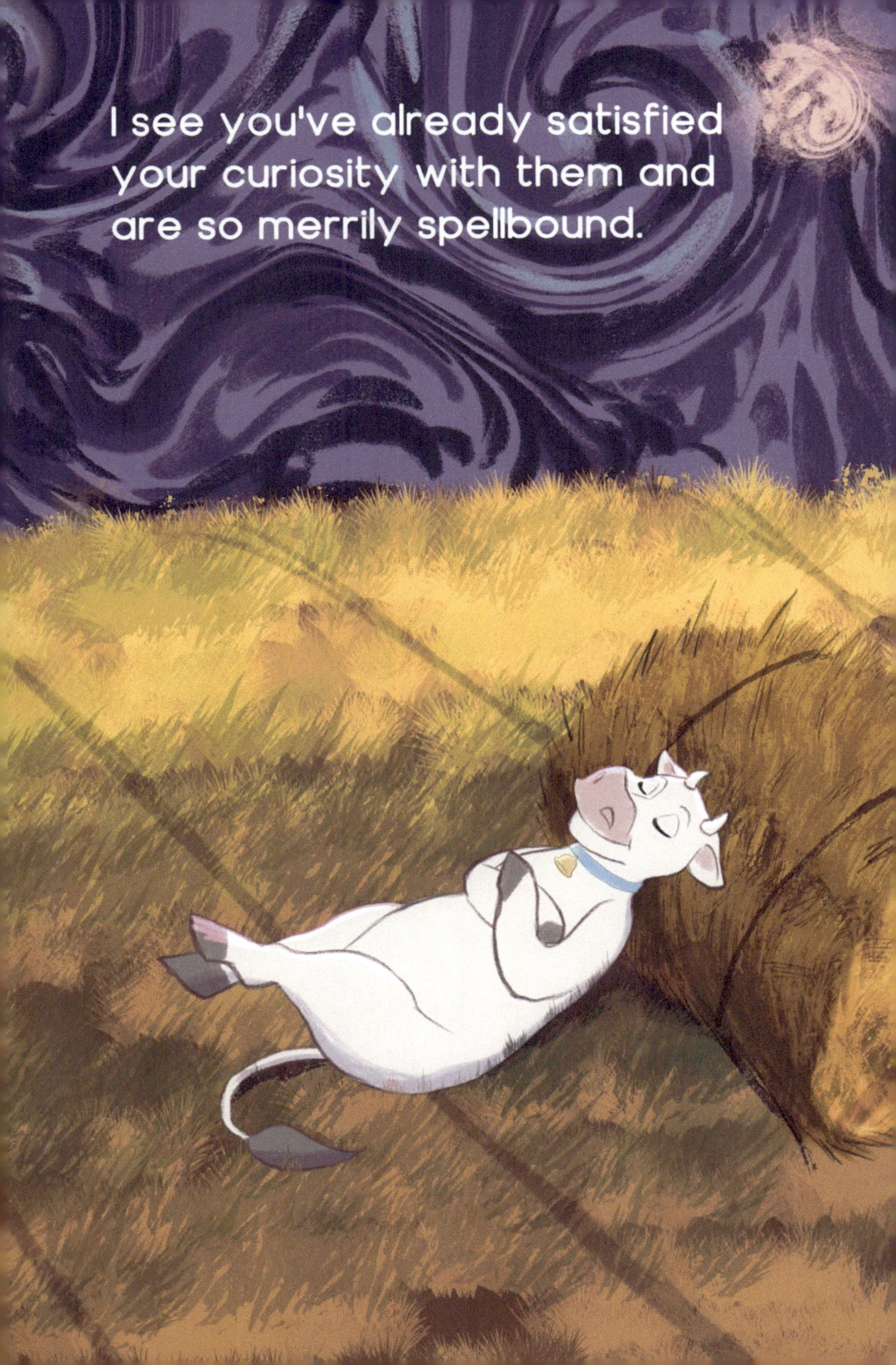

I see you've already satisfied
your curiosity with them and
are so merrily spellbound.

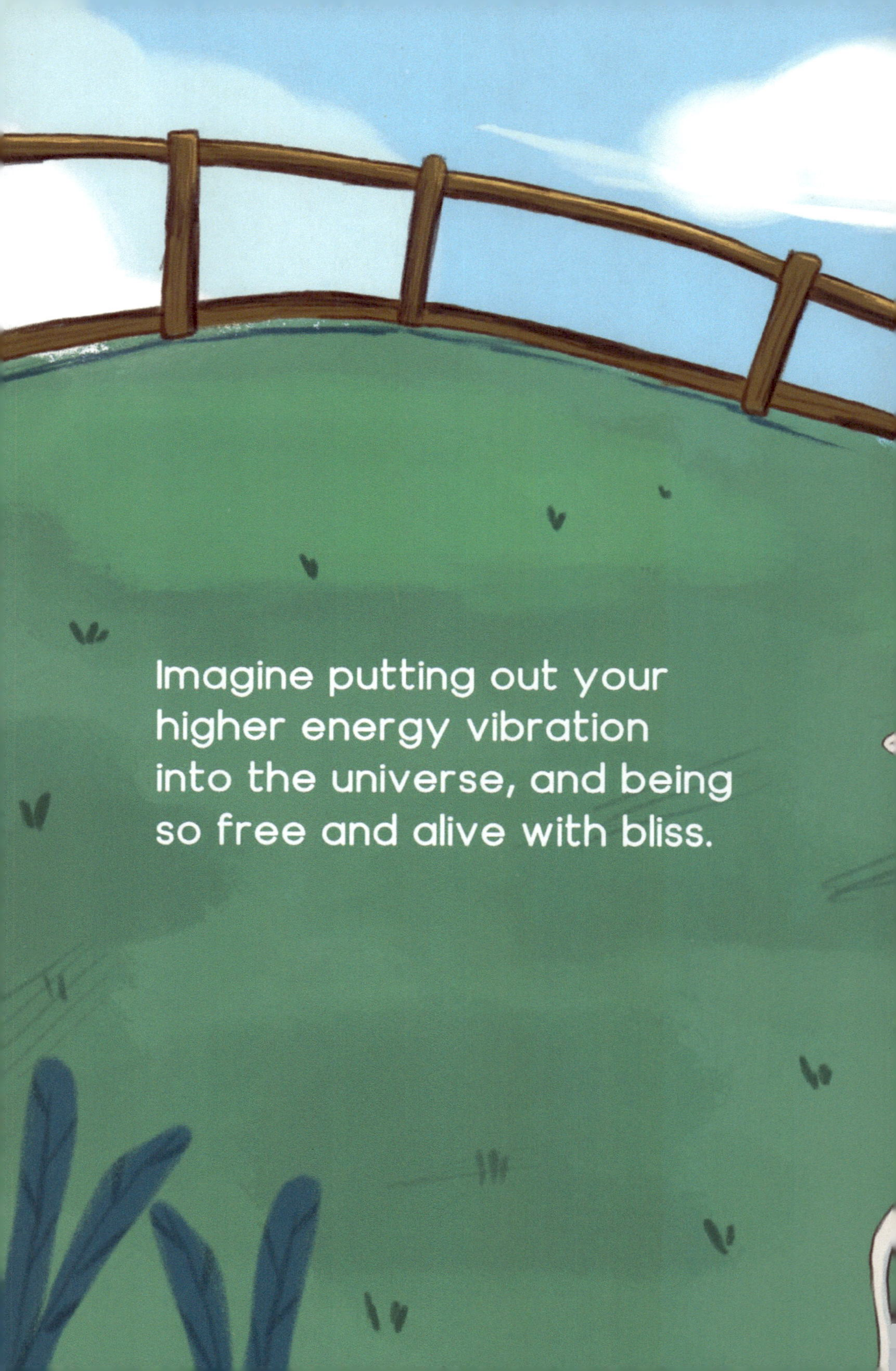

Imagine putting out your higher energy vibration into the universe, and being so free and alive with bliss.

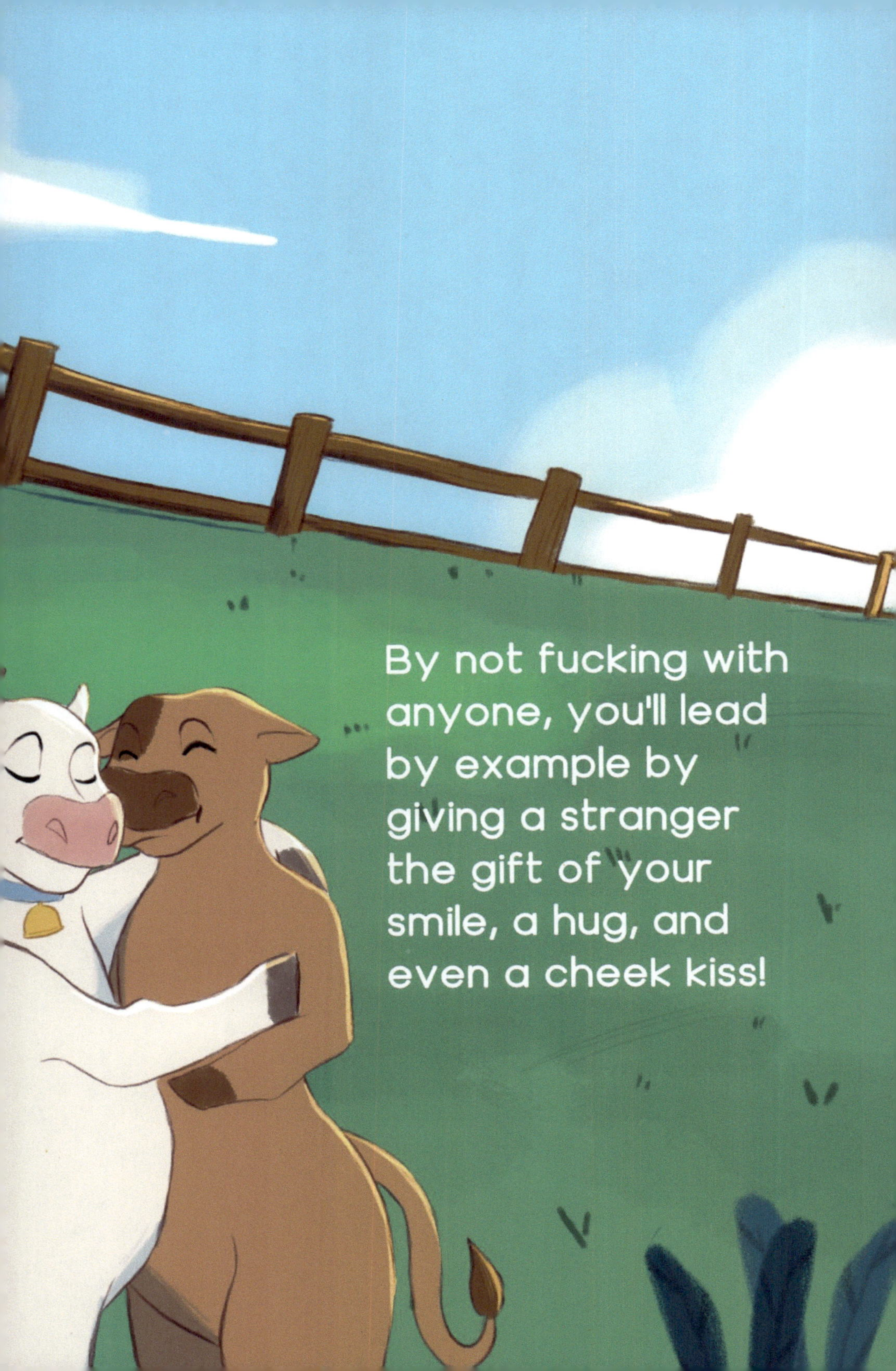
By not fucking with
anyone, you'll lead
by example by
giving a stranger
the gift of your
smile, a hug, and
even a cheek kiss!

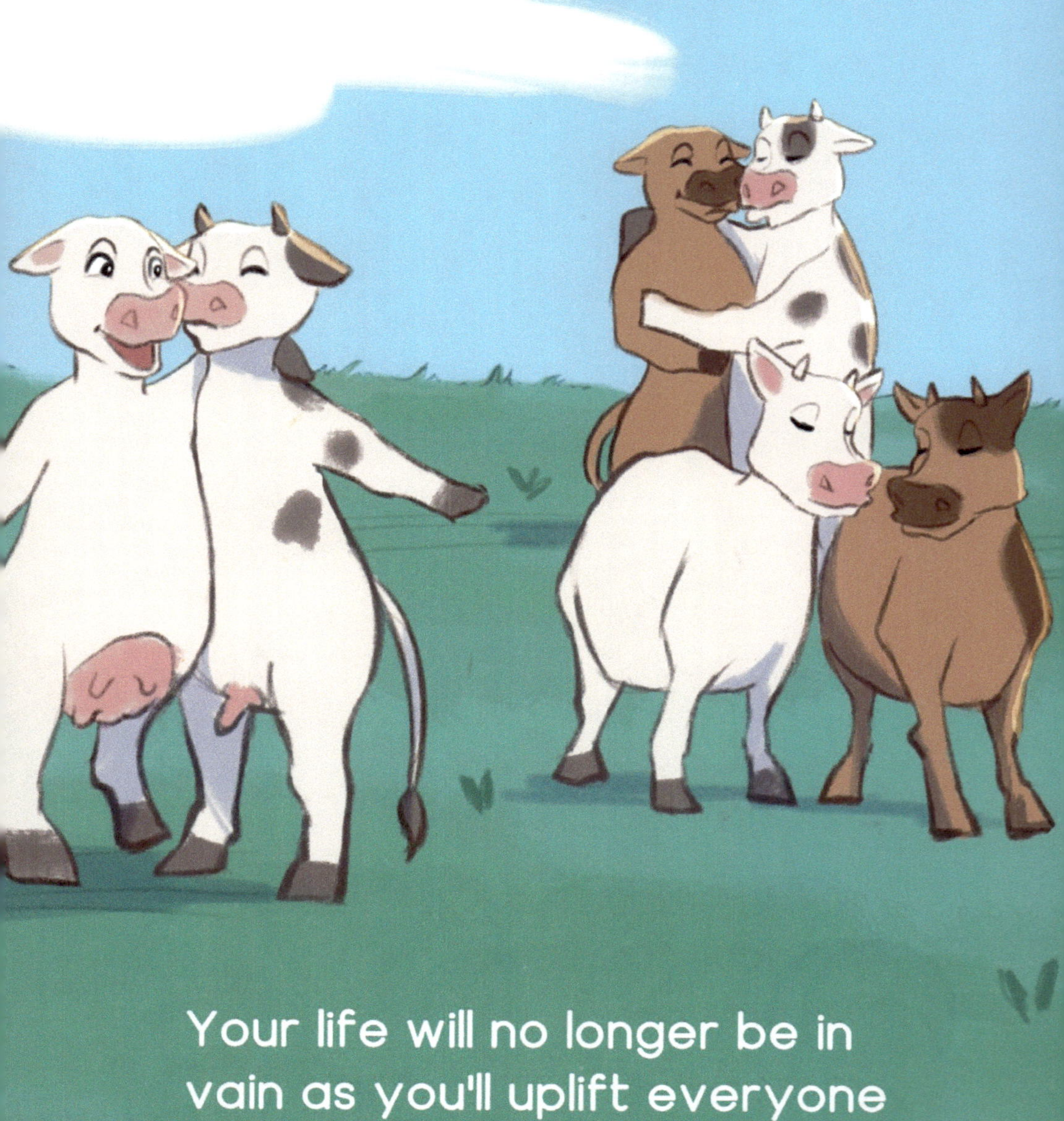

Your life will no longer be in vain as you'll uplift everyone on the farm with the antidote to fear, hatred, greed, ego, division, and other earthly shit.

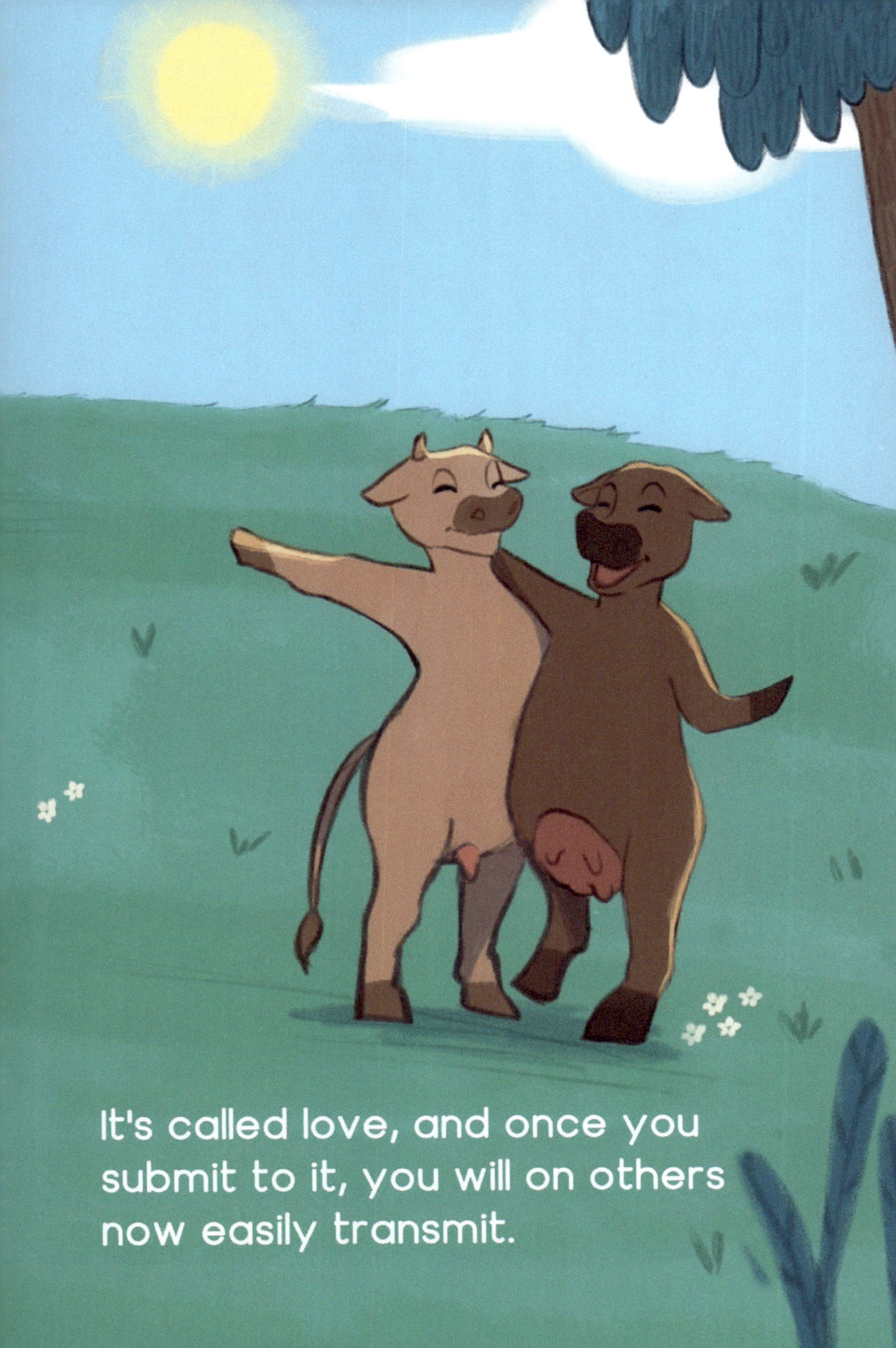

It's called love, and once you submit to it, you will on others now easily transmit.

You see, love fills the soul, heals the heart, and frees the mind.

Especially, when your ass is sick of being full of shit and confined.

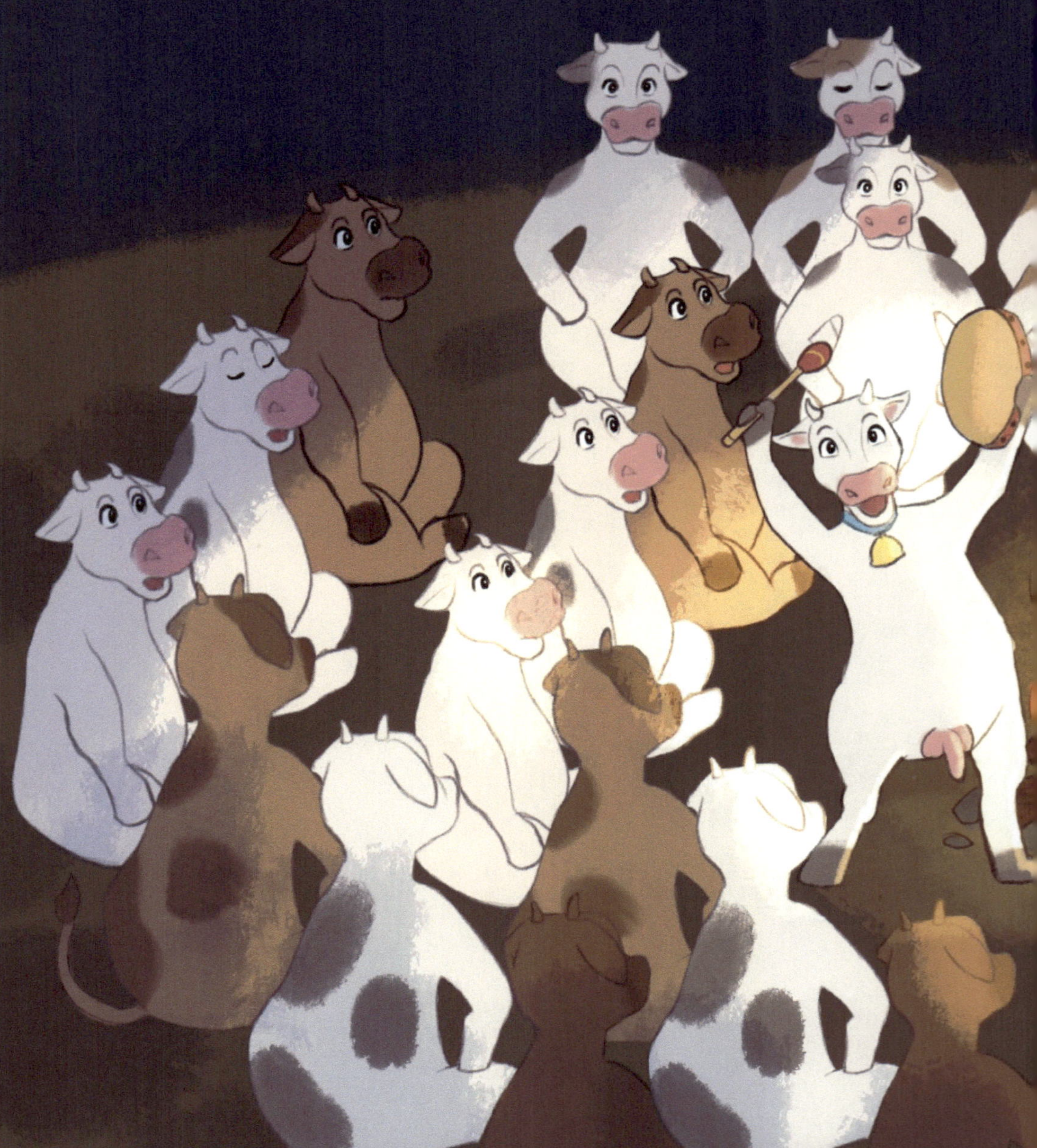

So get up, and keep on drumming to your own different beat dude.

Not giving a fuck to be popular or conventionally understood.

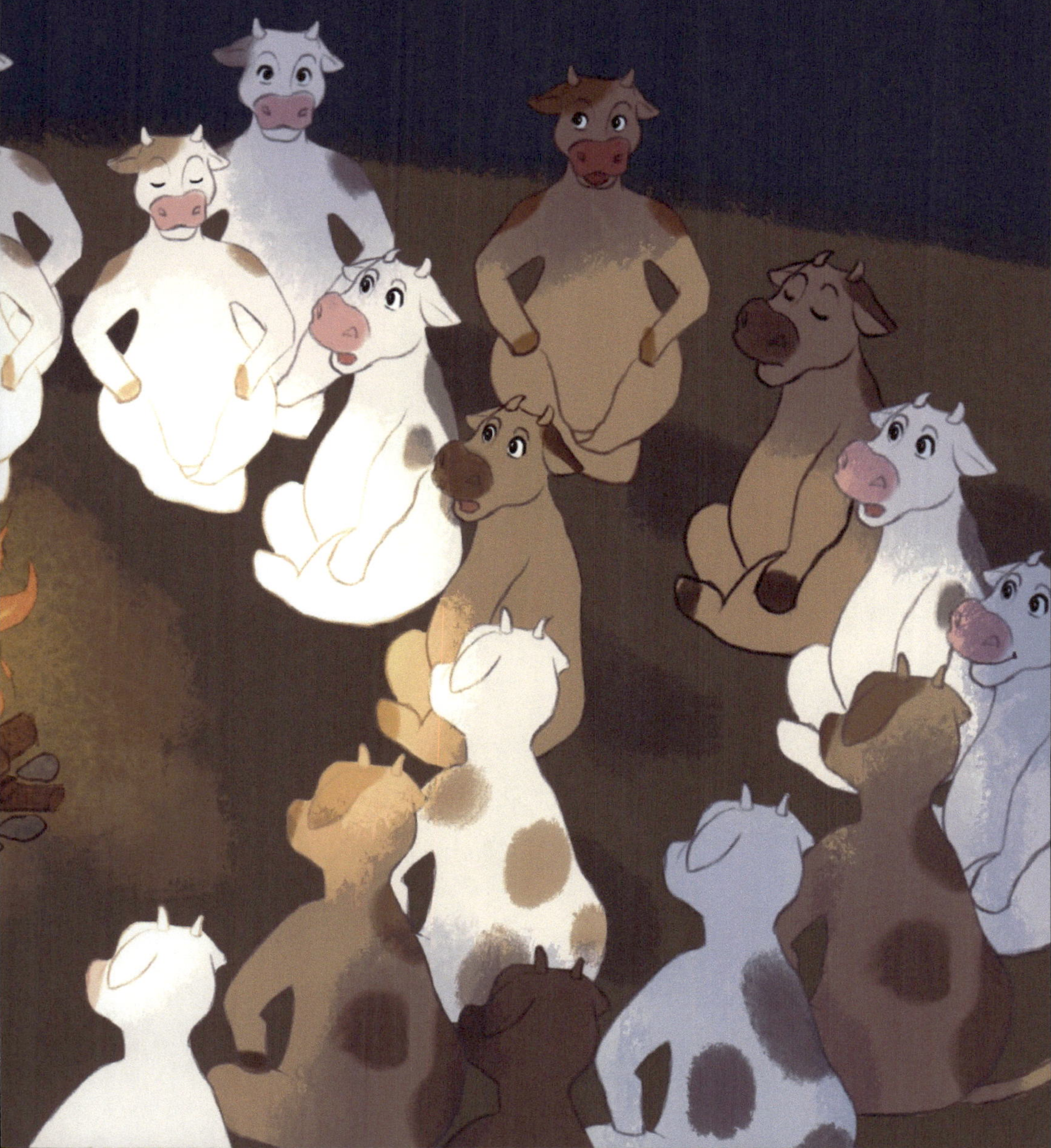

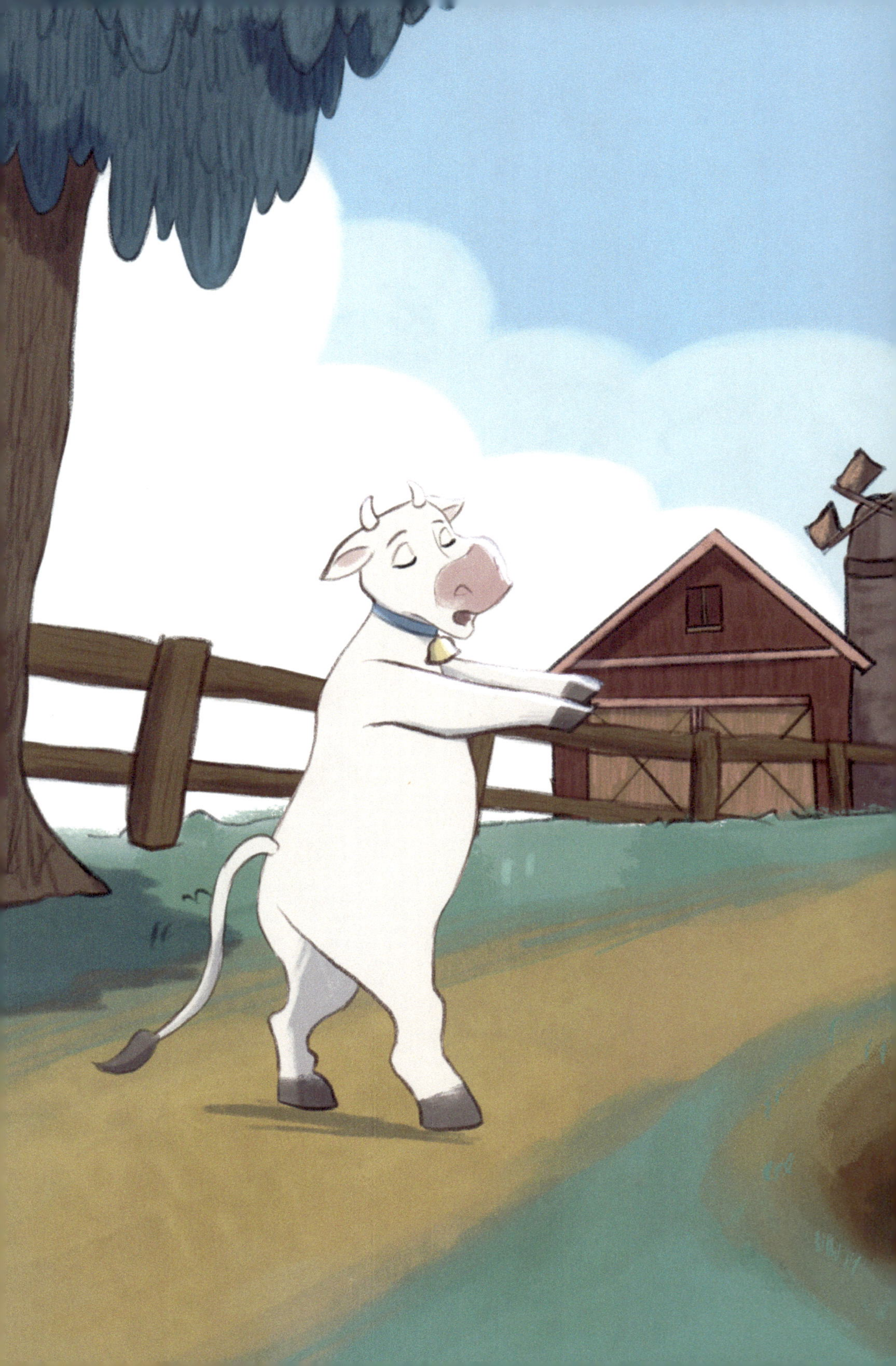

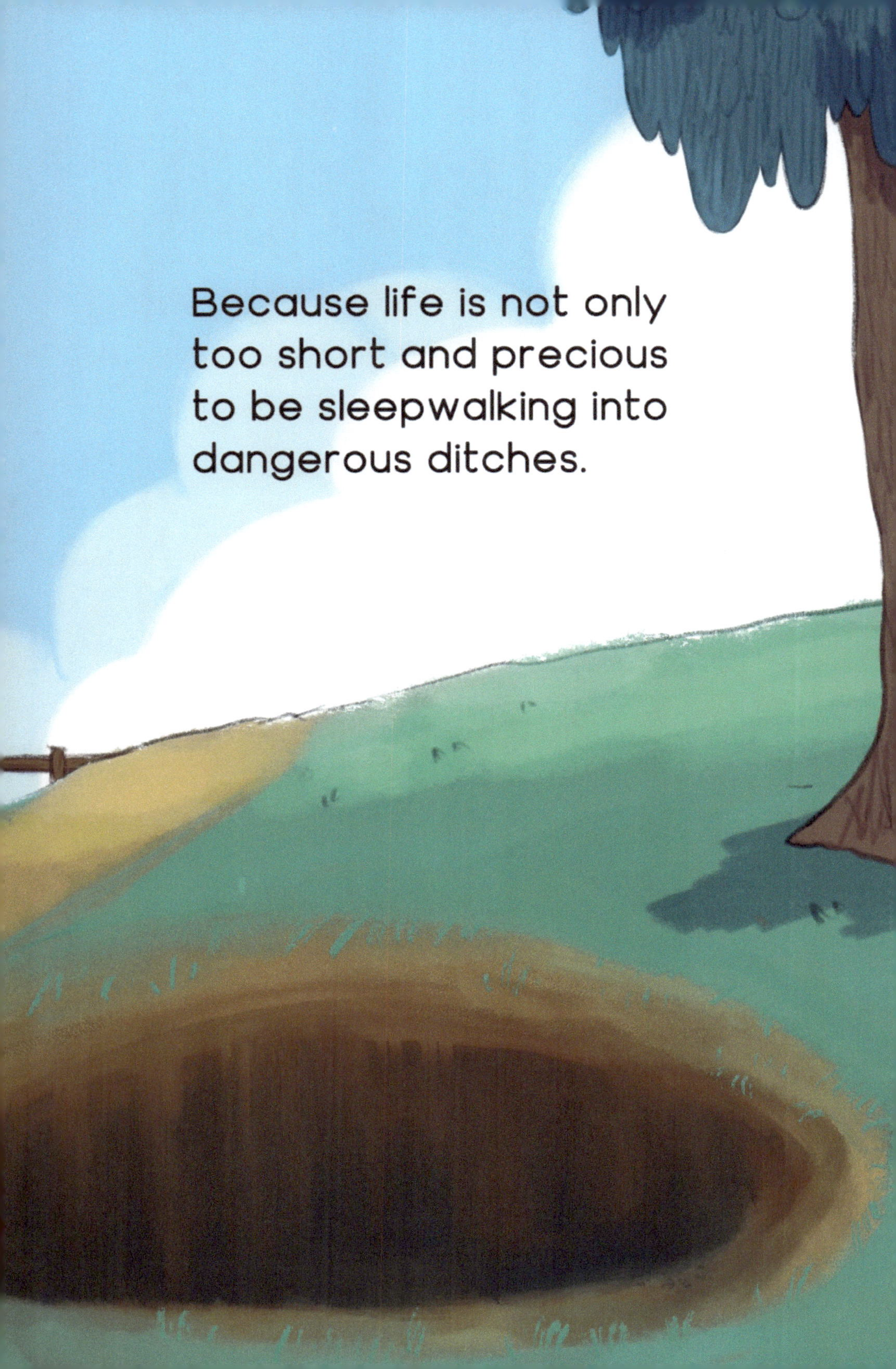

Because life is not only too short and precious to be sleepwalking into dangerous ditches.

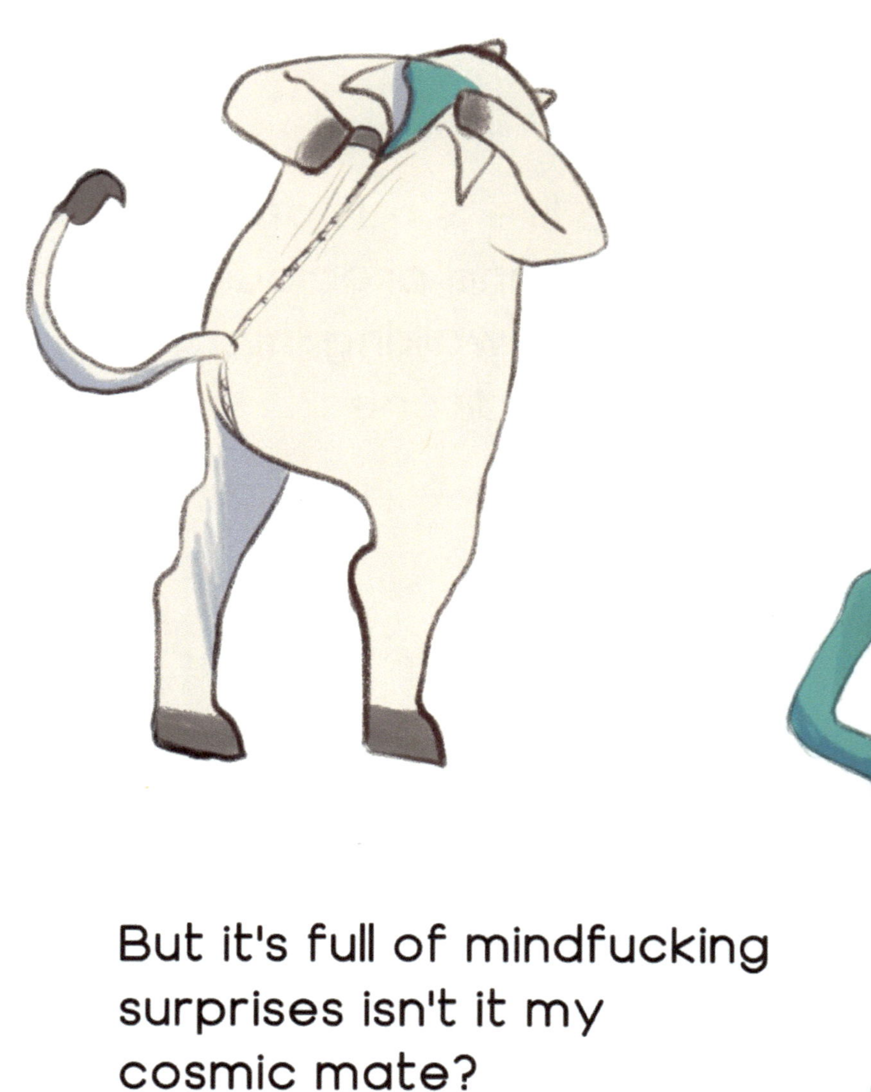

But it's full of mindfucking surprises isn't it my cosmic mate?

So, wake the fuck up now... and don't let your species self-slaughter be its ultimate fate!

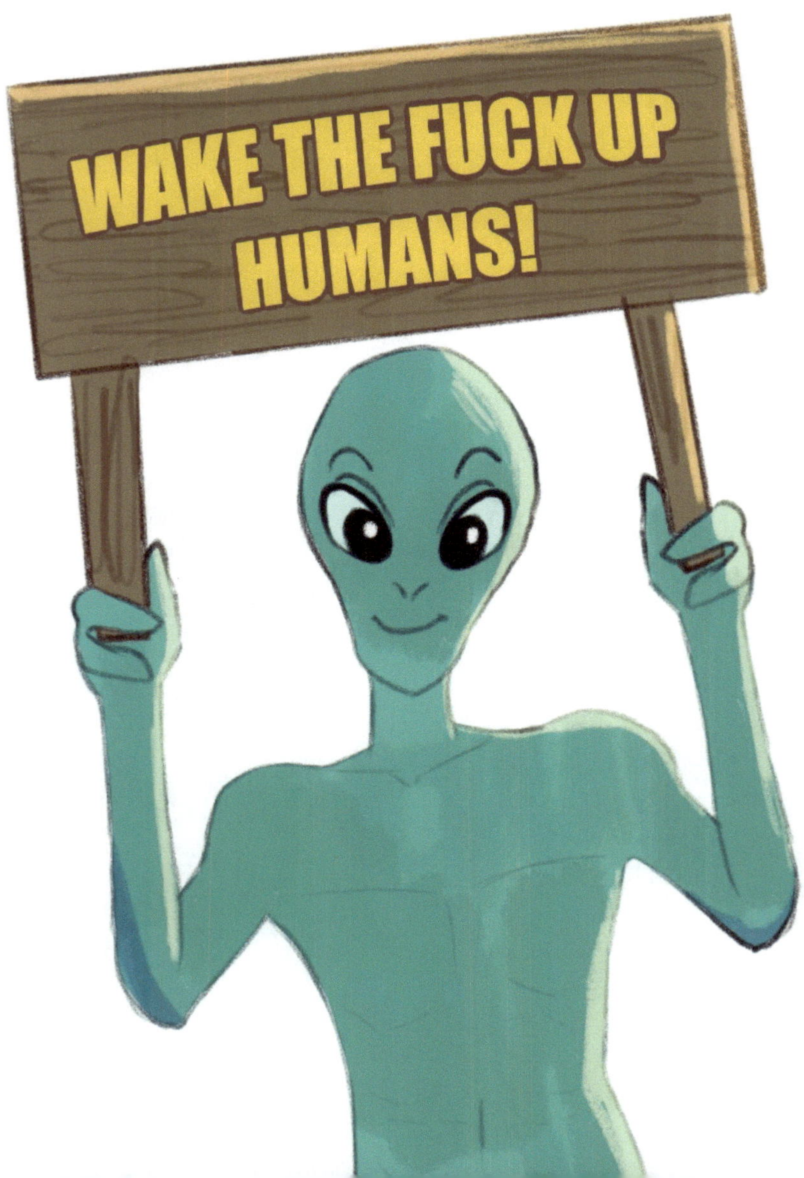

The more you focus on
the distractions and
shiny objects , the less
clearly you'll see the
dark ditch you're in.

- Jim Peera

INSPIRATIONAL SHORT VIDEOS
By Jim Peera

Also, by Jim Peera…

A captivating MEMOIR, a no-nonsense SELF-HELP GUIDE and a creative PEACE PLAN FOR AMERICA:

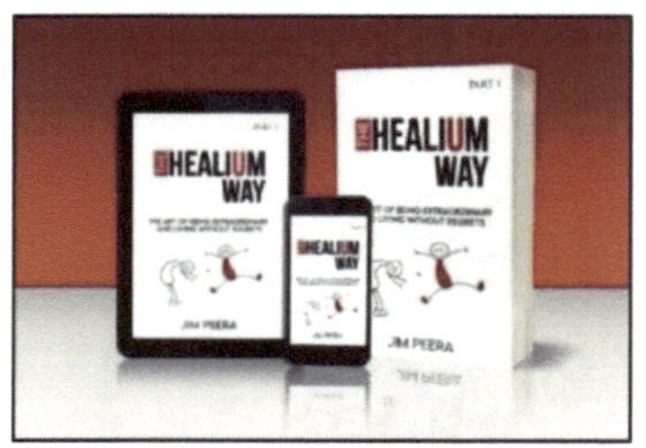

THE HEALIUM WAY

The Art of Being Extraordinary and Living Without Regrets.

Part 1 & 2

"An exciting and interactive 2-Part book filled with art, poetry, exercises and amazing real-life stories".

Read this book and get *"Healiumized!"*

www.TheHealiumWay.com

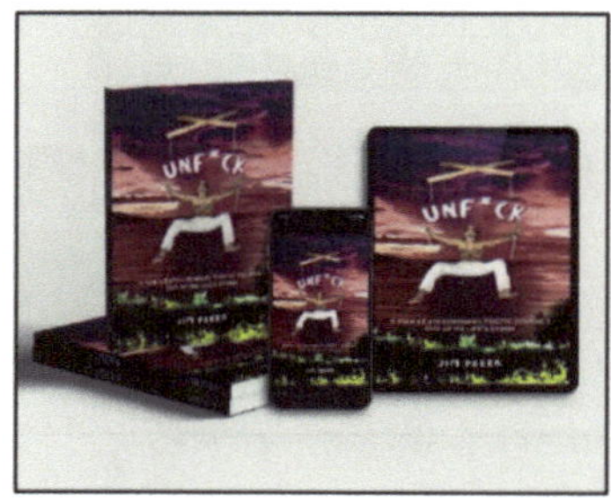

UNF*CK

A Man's Extraordinary POETIC Journey Out of His Life's Storm.

"A WTF love story about a 40-yr heartbreak."

***Includes a must-watch mind-blowing 4- minute selfie-video!**

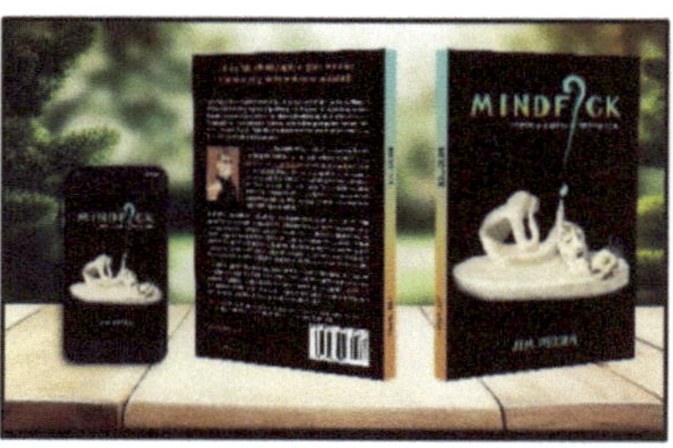

MINDF?CK

Poetry & Art to Free the Soul.

"63 Original Poems w/ Matching Art and Photography!"

www.JimPeera.com

About the Author

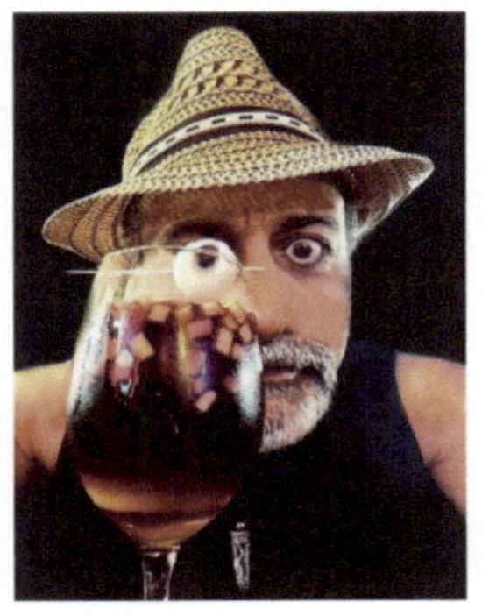

Jim Peera (born Azim Peera), has been called everything from a counterculture renaissance man, to a humorist, and even a 'hypstic' (a hippie-mystic). His life's resume is quite impressive as a non-conformist creative, accomplished entrepreneur, inventor, real-estate developer, property rights defender, artist/healer, author, poet, world traveler, and warrior of peace.

As a man who dislikes labels or identifying himself with anything, he prefers to be known simply as 'a work-in-progress-human.'

Jim founded the nonprofit interactive wellness-with-the-arts project; Healium Center Foundation in Atlanta, Georgia in 2014. He also self-published a 2-part memoir and self-help book: *'The Healium Way: The art of being extraordinary and living without regrets.'* in 2022. In 2023, he published two original poetry books: *'Unf*ck; A man's extraordinary poetic journey out of his life's storm'* and '*Mindf?ck; Poetry and art to free the soul.'*

Mr. Peera has lived a full and adventurous life and his journey hasn't been short of being *extra*ordinary. Being true to himself, he has always believed in living a life of balance with the medicine of the creative and healing arts as his uplifting drug. In addition to sculpting, photography, film-making, sound healing, and drumming; poetry has always been his favorite outlet for self-expression and social commentary.

The multi-dimensional American immigrant from Tanzania, East Africa is a well-rounded spiritual family man with two grown children and a wife of forty-two years. He has lived in France, England, Costa Rica and currently resides in the U.S A.

For more information visit him at:

JimPeera.com

www.ingramcontent.com/pod-product-compliance
Lightning Source LLC
Chambersburg PA
CBHW042201030726
47602CB00005B/85

* 9 7 8 1 7 3 7 5 9 5 0 6 9 *